LOVE
has
a price
tag

ALSO BY ELISABETH ELLIOT

Twelve Baskets of Crumbs

LOVE
has
a price
tag

Elisabeth Elliot

CHRISTIAN HERALD BOOKS
Chappaqua, New York

Library of Congress Cataloging in Publication Data
Elliot, Elisabeth.
    Love has a price tag.

    1. Elliot, Elisabeth. 2. Christian biography—United
States. I. Title.
BR1725.E46A34   248'.2 [B]   79-50944
ISBN 0-915684-87-X

For Miriam Kenyon
my dear friend
a living paradigm of self-giving love

Contents

Introduction

On the wall of my study is a picture of nineteen people in the back yard of an old Philadelphia house. The men stand at the back wearing high stiff collars and short lapels, their hair parted in the middle. The women, wearing long, heavy skirts and fancy shirt-waists, sit with shoulders straight and hands at rest. In their midst is an old patriarch with a long beard. On an Oriental rug spread on the grass sit three boys. The smallest of the boys is my father at two years of age. He is wearing a suit with short pants, black stockings, high buttoned shoes, and an expression of consternation.

This was the Trumbull family. As I look at the picture I am aware of how much has been given and how much will yet be required of me. I also realize that it should not surprise me that I am a writer. There are five writers in the picture—the patriarch himself, my great-grandfather, Henry Clay Trumbull, who was a chaplain in the Civil War and wrote many books; his son, Charles Gallaudet Trumbull, who wrote a booklet called "The

Life That Wins" which sold millions of copies; his son-in-law, Samuel Scoville, a newspaper columnist, naturalist and writer of many boys' books; another son-in-law, Philip E. Howard, my grandfather; and his son, Philip E. Howard, Jr., my father. In addition to writing books and articles, all but Scoville worked on the *Sunday School Times*, a non-denominational weekly. My father followed his Uncle Charlie as editor, and my early recollection is of his striding up Washington Lane from the railroad station in Germantown, a suburb of Philadelphia, carrying a briefcase full of manuscripts which he read in the evenings.

My father kept a dictionary close to the dining room table so that when questions about the meaning and pronunciation of words arose in conversation we could settle them at once. Proper English was required at all times regardless of what we children might be used to hearing from our schoolmates. Although he never wrote anything but the clearest, most straightforward, scripturally-oriented non-fiction, he had a novelist's eye and ear. He noticed things. He would remember the color of the socks of a visitor in his office, or the shape of a dinner guest's thumbs. He could quote exactly what people had said to him and describe with exquisite precision a street scene observed on his way to work. He was an amateur ornithologist and although he had only one eye because of a childhood accident, he could see birds it would take us who had two eyes five minutes to find. He taught us to notice things and to articulate what we saw. For a few years we put out a family newspaper, *Chirps from Birdsong* (Birdsong was the name of our New

Jersey house) which he edited and to which we contributed. He would ask for a poem, a story, a news item, a cartoon from different members of the family, and of course it was an invitation we could not decline. My earliest "published" works appeared in *Chirps*.

There were six of us children, spread over a period of sixteen years, but the oldest three of us remember the Depression. My father earned something in the neighborhood of twenty-five hundred dollars a year. We lived in a "double" house in what is now a slum area of Germantown with a pocket-handkerchief-size yard that seemed to produce hairpins and pearl buttons more readily than grass. We did not know that we were "poor," for in those days the door bell was often rung by peddlers selling shoelaces, needles and thread, or clothesline props. My mother told us not to buy anything but just to give them a dime from the tithe box. My parents were strict tithers, and the box of dimes in the living room table drawer was a portion of the money given to God. Because we were always in the position of givers, we thought we were well off. Treats, however, were very few and therefore very much more appreciated than they seem to be by children today. A Milky Way had to go around for all of us, and I don't suppose we had more than two a year. Saturday afternoon walks at Thomas's Place, a section of Fairmount Park, were special treats when my father would show us birds, imitate their calls, identify ferns and wildflowers, and, best of all, mysteriously "find" Saltines for us in the hollow trunks of trees or behind rocks.

One Valentine's Day Mother put a tiny paper cup

filled with red cinnamon candy hearts by our places at the lunch table. Just before Easter I came home from kindergarten to find a purple-dyed chick peep-peeping in a carton by the heat register in my bedroom. On the morning after my father's return from leading a tour to Palestine for the *Sunday School Times* I awoke to find a carved olive-wood donkey on the chair by my bed. These surprises were highlights of my childhood because they were, of necessity, rare. The gratitude thus learned is a lasting blessing perhaps often missed by those who "have everything."

In our neighborhood there were forty-two boys and only one girl besides myself. I steered clear of her because our family regarded her family's religion as highly dangerous. She steered clear of me because she had a tyrannical grandfather who shouted at her as soon as she got out of sight. Occasionally I was allowed to play with the boys, my brothers among them, or to join their "sled-wagon" trains careening down McCallum Street hill. But I spent a good deal of time alone.

I was excessively shy, partly because I was always very tall for my age. In an elegant hotel lobby in Atlantic City one day a little girl raced across the room to ask me how old I was. My mortification was complete when she raced back again shrieking, "Granny, Granny, that great big girl over there is only seven years old!" On visits to my father's office I dreaded people's saying, "Why, how you've grown! Soon you'll be just like your father!" He was six feet three.

My parents were highly disciplined. My father would rise at 4:30 or 5:00 to read the Bible and pray for us. My mother kept an immaculate house, served meals on time, prayed with each child at bedtime. Their habitual discipline of themselves enabled them also to discipline us. We recognized that they were always in charge. Rules were not negotiable. Our opinions were not polled. This was their house, and as long as we lived in it we knew we were expected to do things their way.

My mother kept a small switch handy in each room, usually on the lintel of the door. Any disobedience could be quickly corrected—often by the mere raising of her eyes to the top of the door.

We had family devotions not once but twice daily. These included hymn singing, Bible reading and prayer. We were encouraged to study the Bible for ourselves and practice private devotion. We went to church, Sunday school, young people's meetings, missionary meetings—whatever was going on at the church. We read missionary books and we entertained missionaries in our home. My parents had been missionaries for five years in Belgium, where I was born. (We came back to the States when I was five months old.)

Not long ago, after a meeting in which I had described my homelife, a man wrote to me, "I'm sure glad I'm not your brother. I could never have taken that kind of rigidity." I had failed to mention the fun we had. My father would tell stories till the tears of laughter rolled down my mother's face. We children enjoyed them and enjoyed one another. It was a happy home. We knew we were loved, we knew the Lord was the head of our house, we knew where the lines were drawn, we were safe. I am sure that to understand God's chastening as a necessity of his love has been easier for me, coming from such a home, than it would be for one who has known only that feeble human sentiment called love to which discipline is opposed.

When any of us complained of jobs we were asked to do or of conditions not to our liking, another would be sure to remind us that this was "G.M.T." Good Missionary Training. It was taken for granted that even if we did not become foreign missionaries, we needed the same rigorous training. As it turned out, four of the six have been foreign missionaries.

When my father was promoted to editor on the death of his uncle, there was enough money to allow me to attend a private Christian boarding school. It was there that the things I had been taught at home began to come into focus. Sometimes one has "ears to hear" from outsiders the home truths he has heard all his life but to which his ears were closed: "Don't go around with a Bible under your arm if you can't sweep under your bed." "What you are now is what you are. It's those tiny little things in your life which, if you don't correct them now, will crack you up when you get out of this school." I was encouraged to write—poetry for special occasions, copy for the school paper and yearbook, speeches and readings. I was required to get up on a platform and give monologues and declamations and to participate in formal debates. I began to try to think things through, to clarify alternatives, and to shape ideas into words.

I graduated from that school with most of the available honors. I was among other things valedictorian—of a class of ten. At Wheaton College I was a very small frog in a very big puddle, but I managed to keep on writing from time to time. I was a cub reporter on the college newspaper and I joined a writers' club. I remember attending only one meeting. Each of us read something to be publicly criticized, and the judgment on my offering—a poem, I think it was—was so devastating I am not sure I ever went back. I managed to work my way up to the varsity debate squad, dealing with scintillating subjects such as free trade and compulsory arbitration. My colleague was Liz Rice, one of the five long-haired daughters of John R. Rice, author of *Bobbed Hair, Bossy Wives, and Women Preachers.* We had our shining hour in 1947 when we won some sort of a debate championship in a Minnesota tournament. I quit while I was ahead and joined the glee club. Because of the traveling required, debating and singing did not mix.

One week before I graduated, a junior from Oregon named Jim Elliot, who had been sitting beside me in Greek classes and studying Thucydides with me in the hall outside the library, got around to admitting that he was in love with me. Marriage, however, was not a possibility, it seemed. He was convinced that God wanted him to be single like the apostle Paul, at least until he had been in jungle missionary work for long enough to determine whether a wife would be a liability or an asset. It was five and a half years before we got a green light from God to be married, five and a half years of learning to trust him with what matters most, of walking by faith and not by sight, of believing the promise of Psalm 84: "no good thing will he withhold from them that walk uprightly."

During that interval I studied linguistics at the University of Oklahoma, took a year of Bible school, worked as a home missionary in Alberta for a summer, got a job as a clerk in a fancy women's specialty shop in Philadelphia, tutored two missionary kids in New Jersey, taught public speaking in a high school, spent a few months living in a cheap apartment in Brooklyn while I tried to learn some Spanish from Puerto Ricans, and at last found myself in Quito, Ecuador, learning Spanish by living in a home where no English was spoken. After six months in Quito and nine months in the west jungle working on a tribal language which had never before been written down, I went to the "Oriente," the east jungle, to learn yet another language. Jim Elliot was working with Quichuas, and had asked me to marry him—"but not until you learn Quichua," he added. My motivation was powerful. I learned it—at least well enough to get by—and we were married by the equivalent of a justice of the peace in the capital city. Jim was not much for ceremony of any kind, having grown up in a "Plymouth Brethren" family, so we agreed that we could do without the fuss of a wedding, especially since we had neither family nor close friends to share it with us.

"Lo, this is our God, we have waited for him," was the verse given us on our wedding day. We could not have waited in peace had we known that our marriage would last only twenty-seven months. But God gives us our "daily bread," enough grace for a day at a time. When Jim died in January of 1956 the grace was there. He had gone with four missionary friends to take the gospel to a tribe called Auca, but they were taken for cannibals and speared to death.

Books were asked for then. The whole world was

interested in that story, and that is how I began to write. I was a missionary before I married Jim and there was no reason to stop being a missionary when he died. I went ahead with the work we had been doing in the Quichua tribe, fitting in the writing wherever I could find the time. An opportunity came to go and live with the Aucas—I had "asked for it," I had prayed, "Lord, if there's anything you want me to do about them, show me, I'm yours," and he took me up on it. Of course I did not really expect him to. I was a widow with a ten-month-old child. What could I do that five men did not do? But we went. Rachel Saint, the sister of one of the missionaries killed, went too. After two years in an Auca settlement Valerie and I went back to the Quichuas, then returned to the States for her schooling when she reached fourth grade.

The miracle that could never happen happened in 1969 when I remarried. I had thought it was a miracle to marry the first time. To imagine a second was beyond me. Addison Leitch was a college professor and writer, a man of great good humor and intelligence, though he rejected the name of scholar. "I'm a pointer and an explainer," was his claim. "It's my job to say 'Do you see this? Do you know what it means?' " He took a position teaching theology at Gordon-Cornwell Seminary in Massachusetts. We both wrote books and articles and sometimes even took speaking engagements as a team. When asked what he liked to do in his spare time, Add said "Curl up with a good author!" Writing was recreation for Add. He found it difficult to imagine how I could labor so arduously over my *Christian Herald* column every other month. I would spend days on it. For the column he wrote for *Christianity Today* he would set aside a morning, sit down in any easy chair, dictate it into a machine, and have a secretary transcribe it. Rarely did he alter a word. His last book, *This Cup*, was on suffering. Not long after it appeared he found he had cancer. We had ten months left before he died, ten months of medical tests and treatments, of prayers and anointings and hopes kindled and extinguished.

Four more years of widowhood followed and then the third miracle—Lars Gren, a former salesman who in middle life decided that was not the way he wanted to spend the rest of it, and came to seminary to prepare for Christian service. If ever there was a "one-man woman" I thought it was I, but each milestone of my life has entailed the breaking up of categories. A third husband, Lord? I couldn't believe this was what God meant, but the Lord knows how to get through to us when we honestly want to know what he wants. As I prayed and pondered the decision, the Holy Spirit brought to my attention words from 1 Corinthians 12, "Men have different gifts, but it is the same Lord who accomplishes his purposes through them all." Gradually it became perfectly clear that Lars was a part of God's purpose for me. He was a gift God had been trying to give me, but it took awhile to get my attention and to shuffle my categories again from widow to wife, from saying "I" to saying "we." We were married in 1977.

The whole purpose of life, I believe, is to learn to know God. "This is life eternal," John wrote, "that they might know thee." In each of the "crises" of my own life I have looked for God's meaning, and have sought to learn of him. A prayer given to me by my grandfather Howard, written by Phillips Brooks, has become a part of the fabric of all my prayers: "O Lord, by all thy dealings with us, whether of joy or pain, of light or darkness, let us be brought to thee. Let us value no treatment of thy grace simply because it makes us happy or because it makes us sad, because it gives us or denies us what we want; but may all that thou sendest us bring us to thee, that, knowing thy perfectness, we may be sure in every disappointment that thou art still loving us, and in every darkness that thou are still enlightening us, and in every enforced idleness that thou art still using us; yea, in every death that thou art still giving us life, as in his death thou didst give life to thy Son, our Savior, Jesus Christ. Amen."

I believe God answers prayer. He is answering this prayer. But he is not finished. He is bringing me with patience and gentleness to himself. Jesus promised that to the man who loves and obeys, the Father will make himself known. The essays in this book spring from the incidents of everyday life and my effort to answer Add's questions: Do you *see* this? Do you know what it *means*? I try to see things clearly. I ask God to show me what he sees in them. I seek his meaning, for in the last analysis true spiritual understanding is not an achievement of the intellect but the divine reward for love and obedience. And, though unconditional love has a price tag, what a bargain price it is for such a reward. "Then my Father will love him and we will come to that man and make our home within him" (Phillips).

Author's Note

This collection, first published as a bi-monthly column in *Christian Herald* magazine, is arranged chronologically to preserve the continuity of my life's experiences. Occasional repetition of ideas has been allowed to stand—one's thoughts do have a way of recurring.

Animals, My Kinsmen

While driving recently I was listening to one of those "call-in" shows on the radio, and was glad to hear a question that had nothing to do with politics or abortion or the drug problem. A lady wanted to know whether mongrels were ever trained to be seeing-eye dogs. She felt sorry for all those mongrels she saw on the streets, and she thought it would be so nice if they could be trained to help blind people because (and here the host had to ask her to repeat what she had said to make sure he had heard it right) it would give them something to look forward to.

Just exactly what view did the lady take of the minds of dogs? Did they suffer identity crises? Were they bored with life on the streets, finding that there wasn't much future in it?

Then I heard a recording of the songs of whales. I wouldn't have believed it if I had not just read the fascinating article in the *New Yorker* by Faith McNulty, "Lord of the Fish," in which she says that whales do indeed "sing." A man named Frank Watlington, an engineer with the Columbia University Geophysical Field Station at Bermuda, recorded the songs with a hydrophone. In contrast to birdsongs, which are light and quick, the song of the whale is heavy and slow, a sort of muted trumpeting interspersed with ratcheting and at times with a surprisingly high, thin whining. It is jubilant and boisterous, eerie and sorrowful, often reminding one of an echo. I had the feeling the whale sometimes experimented with different kinds of sound and when pleased with one drew it out, then abruptly reverted to the ones he'd practiced before, even including a loud, rude Bronx cheer.

The question naturally arises as to why whales make these noises. "It must be the mating call," is the first suggestion most people come up with. But that theory doesn't stand up to scientific investigation. The truth is that nobody has figured out why whales make the noises they make. But then, as my husband pointed out, nobody has figured out why human beings make the noises they make either. Miss McNulty believes whales sing so they won't be alone.

I know a Vermont policeman who was on duty as a game warden one day during hunting season. He sat quietly in the woods and heard a stirring in the leaves over a little rise and soon a young bear appeared about thirty yards away. The bear lay down on his side and squirmed around in a circle in the dead leaves, pushing them into a pile in the center of the circle. Then he climbed a tree and jumped into the pile. He did this not once but again and again. Obviously he was having fun.

I have always found animals irresistible. The whole idea of a kingdom of beings utterly separate and distinct from ourselves who nevertheless gaze upon us and think thoughts about us ravishes me. What do they mean? Why are they there? What did God mean by making them? When he made man, he made him in his own image. When he made animals, his imagination ranged wide and free. But we confront them, we breathe the same air and walk the same earth and live and move and have our being in the same Creator. So we seek to understand them, and quite naturally we ascribe to them our own passions and needs—the ambition of the forsaken mongrel who roams the streets, hoping for some useful niche in the scheme of things; the loneliness of the tremendous beast that moves through dark oceans, singing his wistful song on the offchance that there will be ears to hear; the gaiety of the little yearling bear who, all alone, makes his arrangement for joy and then joyfully climbs, plunges, plays and climbs again.

These creatures are, I suppose, unaware (but perhaps I am wrong—perhaps they are profoundly aware) that a human heart goes out, a human ear is tuned, a human eye watches. And perhaps animals are aware of the divine heart and ear and eye. Perhaps they are not so oblivious as we. Even young lions, according to the Psalmist, "seek their food from God." Look at the face of a good dog. There is simplicity and gentleness and reverence in those liquid eyes. Does he behold the face of the Father? It is easy for me to believe that he does.

God meant the animals to instruct us. I am sure that is one of the things he meant. When he had listened to all the arguments and complaints of his servant Job, and all the bombast of his friends, he answered by the revelation of himself. And this revelation, beginning with the dimensions of the universe, the mighty harmony of the morning stars, the phenomena of sea, clouds, snow, hail, rain, dew, hoarfrost, ice and the constellations, wound up with animals.

What Job didn't know then was that God had already identified himself with one of his own creatures, the gentlest, most harmless little animal of all. He was a Lamb, slain from the foundation of the world.

I have often thought that that terrible ash heap on which poor Job scratched and shrieked would have been made so much more endurable if he had had the least inkling of that. He was overpowered, but had he any idea at all of how he was loved? I have been comforted, in the midst of what seemed to me like ashes, by the thought of the Lamb, and even (does it seem absurd?) by the unflagging attention and affection of a little black dog. For I remember that when Jesus was tempted in the wilderness he had two comforters—angels and animals. The record says he was "with the wild beasts," which I once took to mean he was endangered by them as well as tempted by Satan. I now think otherwise. The animals were surely no threat to him. They kept him company in his sore struggle.

When the impact of life seems about to break us, we can put our minds for a few minutes on fellow creatures—the whale, the bear, or things that "take life blithely, like birds and babies," as Martin Luther said— and remember that there is a sacrifice at the heart of it all. The Lamb became the Shepherd, bearing and caring for the sheep, laying down his life for them both as shepherd and as Lamb, and, in the end, the Book of the Revelation promises, "the Lamb in the midst of the throne shall be their Shepherd, and he will guide them to springs of living water, and God shall wipe away every tear from their eyes."

To Walk Where
Jesus Walked

For as long as I can remember I did not want to go to the Holy Land. I suppose the main reason was those monochromatic slides we used to have to look at in Sunday school. My heart would sink when I learned that somebody was going to show pictures of Palestine. All you saw were little square sand-colored houses and sand-colored camels and lots of sand-colored landscapes that were mostly desert and a lot of people dressed in long robes that reminded me of our Sunday school Christmas plays with everybody wearing bathrobes and towels wrapped around their heads. The whole thing of seeing what were called "holy places" and walking today where Jesus walked and visiting ruins failed to find a response in me.

But seven years ago, just after the Six-Day War, I was persuaded to go to Jerusalem, and now I'm going back again. Israel in 1967 was a place of tremendous excitement and tremendous sadness. There were those who had conquered and those who had just been conquered. There was rubble where the wall had divided the Old City from the New, rubble where villages had been demolished and rubble at the Wailing Wall. I do not expect to find everything sorted out and peaceful when I return. Problems persist which seem to have no possible human solution, and I know from correspondence with friends that all is not as we read in the newspapers. But Jerusalem is a city set apart, a city often besieged and often recovered, which holds at its heart certain treasures that its wars and sins have not yet obliterated.

I had not been at all prepared for the impact that Jerusalem had upon me. I was overpowered. It was in this city, inside and outside its walls, that the events took place which altered the whole course of history. The Crucifixion, said Dorothy Sayers, was after all "the only thing that ever really happened." I knew all of this before I went, of course, but I simply was not prepared for what it did to me when I finally actually stood on that ground.

Christian tourists are often put off by the commercialization of the holy places. You go into the Church of the Holy Sepulchre to find that it is claimed by four different kinds of Christians who get along so badly that the keys to the church have had to be entrusted, it is said, to a Moslem family. There are guides, licensed and unlicensed, clamoring to show you around. There are priests in varied garb waiting at each sacred site with offering boxes; candles are on sale, and the whole place seems dark, dusty and crowded with the trappings of religion.

I would not have expected to like this scene, but I found myself totally captivated. There was something about the crumbling, discolored stone with Crusader's crosses carved into it, the fragrance of the incense and the dim light of the swinging oil lamps that convinced me here was the place, here was concentrated the attention and the devotion—fierce as it sometimes was—of the ages. Christians of all varieties had converged on this place, crowding into it every possible symbol of their hope and longing as well as the unavoidable evidence of their corruption; and that very corruption added its own weight to the meaning of that cross and that empty sepulchre—"for where sin abounded grace did much more abound."

To go to the Garden of Gethsemane, across the Brook Kidron from the Old City, and to know that it was Jesus' custom often to leave the crowded, noisy city and cross that brook and go to where the old olive trees grew on a hillside, was another experience that overwhelmed me. The shape of the city, viewed from that perspective, has not changed very much, I suppose, from the time of Jesus. The shape of the hills surrounding it, the aspect of the valley, the beauty of the olive trees, would be just what Jesus knew. This was the quiet place to which he went when he knew that his hour had come. It was beneath some of these very trees perhaps (for some of them are two thousand years old) that the Son of man struggled with his own fear of death and with the will of the Father.

Over the door of the Basilica of the Agony, which is one name for the church in the Garden, these Latin words are inscribed: SUSTINETE HIC ET VIGILATE MECUM, "Wait here and watch with me." I myself had gone to the Garden several different times during my weeks in Jerusalem, and tried to reconstruct the awful scene: Christ in an agony of conflict and suffering, while the three who had been specially chosen to be with their Master at the end were not doing the one thing he had asked them to do—watch—but were sound asleep. When I was there the sun shone on the soft stone of the city walls and on the brilliant bougainvillea that grew near-by. Buses ground up the hill, taxis honked, tourists rushed by taking pictures, and a group of *kibbutzniks* waving blue and white flags poured out of a bus and passed the Garden without so much as a sideways glance.

It is not our experiences which in the final analysis change us, it is always and only our responses to those experiences. In any of the holy places I could have responded with cynicism, rejection, even outrage. Their mysterious power then would have been lost on me. I found it possible instead to enter in by faith, giving myself in each place to the One who was there before me and who, despite all that worldly-minded humanity had done to those places, was still there if I sought him.

Near one of the olive trees in Gethsemane one of the Darmstadt Sisters of Mary has put up a small plaque:

O my Father, if it be possible, let this cup pass from me, nevertheless not as I will but as thou wilt. Thou, O Jesus, in the darkness of night and grief, didst utter these words of surrender and trust to God the Father. In gratitude and love I will, in my hours of fear and desolation, say after thee, My Father, I cannot understand what thou art about but in thee do I put my trust.

Those Personality Tests

Aristotle said that the purpose of education is to make the pupil like or dislike what he ought. To be educated is to be able to make distinctions. But we are being educated nowadays to believe that distinctions are to be deplored. What you like or dislike has nothing whatever to do with the object. It's merely a matter of taste.

Edwin Newman is one of the few public figures who clings to the quaint idea that distinctions in language are important. It still matters to him whether hopefully means "with hope" or "I hope that," and whether momentarily means "for a moment" or "in a moment."

Distinctions in dress have become fewer and fewer, for the carefully studied "unstudied" look is adopted by most Americans most of the time, whether they're headed for a hike or a party.

Distinctions of race, color, sex and creed are being obliterated as fast as possible, so that we may become a people without identity—colorless, sexless and faithless.

I went to a conference a couple of weeks ago sponsored by a mission organization. The psychiatrist who screens candidates for that mission administered to the entire audience, purely for their own interest (he said), five of the simpler personality tests which he uses. I, like everybody else, dutifully filled in the blanks. It was my first experience of this sort of thing. Nobody had thought of it as a prerequisite for missionaries back in my day, and my missionary friends at the conference agreed with me that no one of the five of us would have made it to Ecuador if they had.

Each question on the "temperament" test began with words like: "Do you feel," "Are you easily tempted to," "Do you tend to," "Is it difficult for you to," "Do you prefer," "Are you regarded as," "Do you like," "Are you comfortable with," "Do you appear"—every one of them questions for which there could be no absolute answers. The doctor assured us that there were no "right" or "wrong" answers. "It's just a matter of what's right for *you*."

Very soothing. No moral distinctions have any bearing on this test. That was what the psychiatrist was saying. The difference between right and wrong really has nothing at all to do with a person's temperament. A simple matter of "pease porridge hot, pease porridge cold." We're not concerned here with what ought to be but simply with what is. Not with what I ought to like but with what I do like, for whatever reasons. Learning "who I am" requires merely the listing of traits—true enough, I suppose, but is there any place for judgment of them as faults or virtues?

But as it turned out, I was categorized at once by my answers. Distinctions were made, all right, whether the tester chose to call them moral ones or "value judgments" or not. If I admire what, in a less analytical age, were called virtues and am "upset" by what were once called faults, I am classified as "R"—regimented, regular, reserved, rigid. To like punctuality, neatness, thrift and self-discipline is to be regimented. To dislike tardiness, slovenliness, profligacy and self-indulgence is to be hostile. (My "hostility scale" was dangerously high.) To be upset by punctuality, neatness, thrift and self-discipline is not regarded, I found, as any index of hostility but rather of geniality, and to "feel comfortable with" tardiness, slovenliness, profligacy and self-indulgence is to be classified as "Z" which, we were informed, means you've got "zip, zing, zest, and zowie"! The conclusion is that discipline and joy are mutually exclusive. (Not certain that I had understood, I inquired whether a person who is rated "pure R" therefore has *no* zip, zing, zest and zowie. The solemn reply: "That is correct.")

There are a number of questions to be raised about this kind of "testing."

What are the presuppositions which underlie the test questions themselves?

First, that people's behavior is governed by their feelings. For the Christian, at least, this is not necessarily true. If my answer to the question *Are you irritated when someone is late for an appointment?* is yes, this does not always mean that I shout at him when he finally arrives. Paul said, "Be angry and sin not." He said, "Never *act* from motives of rivalry or jealousy."

Jesus said, "Inasmuch as ye have done it unto," not, "Inasmuch as ye have felt it toward one of the least of these. . . . " If I say yes when asked if I find it difficult to discipline myself, this does not mean that I therefore do not discipline myself.

Second, that traits of character are—with two notable exceptions—morally indifferent. We are all conditioned or constituted as we are and therefore O.K. We are told to express ourselves, tell the world how we "really feel," and "hang loose." We need not encourage any course of action on any ground other than our own (even "gut-level") feelings.

But there is one unarguable virtue toward which some effort (I gather) needs to be directed. That is tolerance. And there is one thoroughly damnable fault which must be eradicated. That is intolerance. We are encouraged to be tolerant of just about everything and intolerant of almost nothing. (We are permitted to be intolerant of just one thing—intolerance.)

Do certain kinds of behavior merely receive, or do they also merit, certain kinds of response? Are certain reactions more just or appropriate than others? Are there things which are actually in themselves pleasurable, admirable, likable or tolerable, and other things which are painful, detestable, unlikable and intolerable? The Bible makes clear distinctions. Behavior is not merely a question of taste. It speaks of "the activities of the lower nature," which include sexual immorality, impurity of mind, sensuality, hatred, jealousy, bad temper, rivalry and envy. Nowhere does it admonish us to tolerate such activity. (Loving all others certainly does not imply an inability to distinguish between the lovable and the unlovable. How then could we tell an enemy when we saw one?)

Over against that list is the fruit produced in human life by the Spirit of God: love, joy, peace, patience, kindness, generosity, fidelity, tolerance and self-control. "And no law," the Bible says, "exists against any of them." No law, perhaps, except the norms of the personality testers. They like most of the things in the second list, though they won't stand for too much fidelity or self-control. Qualities such as those reveal a tendency to rigidity and are, by the testers' standards, unlikely to occur in the same list with tolerance. But in the world where one quality of personality is as good as another, what need do we have for peace, patience, kindness and generosity? If I am to repay evil with good I must first discern evil.

The total effect of the tests was to diminish responsibility. I found that I was a "type." Everybody's a type. So there we are. Accept it. Like it. Like all the other types. We're all O.K. No need to condemn anything. No need to feel guilty. Don't distinguish between personality traits; that's a "value judgment" and value judgments are always bad. So what if you're a fidgeter, an underachiever, a social boor, a spendthrift? Don't let it upset you. Nothing matters, finally—a messy house or a clean one, work done or work undone, appointments kept or missed, bills paid or unpaid, health guarded or ruined, feelings soothed or ruffled—just be yourself. Here I am, everybody, good old lovable me. Take me the way I am. Love me. If my habits annoy you, there's something wrong with you, not me. You're the one who needs help. You're "uptight."

But no. As I was driving home, mulling over the whole thing, I saw that it wouldn't do. Of course we're meant to love people. Love bears anything, believes anything, endures anything. But we're not meant to ignore distinctions. I saw that if I need not condemn anything neither need I praise. There is nothing to strive for, nothing to emulate, nothing to prize. "Can you be righteous," Traherne wrote, "unless you be just in rendering to things their due esteem?"

It seemed a frightening thing to me to know that the servants of God might be screened by tests which would place the highest value on being easy on oneself and others. Candidates who were easy to live with simply because nothing really made much difference to them would prove, by these methods, to be most desirable. But when Jesus called disciples he asked them to *deny*— to "give up their right to"—themselves.

Would the apostle Paul have passed those tests? It was he who said, "Endure hardness," "Submit yourselves one to another," "In humility think more of each other than you do of yourselves," "Be strong," "Take your stand," "Live lives worthy of your high calling." He even had the courage to say "Let *my example* be the standard by which you can tell who are the genuine Christians"!

"Here is a last piece of advice," he wrote to the Philippians. "If you believe in goodness and if you value the approval of God, fix your minds on whatever is true and honorable and just and pure and lovely and praiseworthy. Model your conduct on what you have learned from me, on what I have told you and shown you, and you will find that the God of peace will be with you."

Our faculties must be trained by practice and taught by the Spirit of God to make the strong and sharp distinctions so essential to Christian character.

Femininity

My late philosopher-theologian husband used to tell his students that the importance of a thing was in direct ratio to the difficulty of defining it. Last year I asked my students in seminary to write a paper defining masculinity and femininity. They were allowed a maximum of two pages in which to do it, but I told them it would be fine with me if they could manage it in two sentences. (None did.) All of them testified that it was the most difficult assignment of the course.

The difficulty has been exacerbated, I am convinced, by the so-called liberation movement, which starts from the premise that there are no distinctions between the sexes other than the purely biological. It seems a strangely naïve and cramped view of the fundamental differentiation of our human existence, especially in this day when most physicians acknowledge that illnesses involve more than the body, when psychiatrists acknowledge that mental illness may have physical causes, and when any spiritual counselor knows that spiritual problems often affect both mind and body. Why, in this most obvious area of sexual distinction, should we blandly (and preposterously) assert that it has no implications deeper than the physiological?

One Thanksgiving weekend I attended the Evangelical Women's Caucus in Washington, D.C. A few women who had read some of my writings greeted me with an astonished "What are *you* doing *here*?"

"I'm an evangelical woman, am I not?" I said, but of course I knew why they were surprised. The conference was to deal with the question of a "biblical" approach to feminism. Those who attended were expected to be feminists, and I don't belong in that crowd.

I cannot be a "feminist" because, for one thing, I believe in femininity—a category which I see as infinitely deeper than the merely physical, a quality radically distinct from masculinity.

I listened in vain for the word *femininity* in any of the major addresses, and I looked in vain for any workshop which might touch on the subject. What women feel, what women want, what women do and what they want to do and don't want to do were all discussed with enthusiasm and even with passion, but what women *are* simply escaped everybody's notice. One workshop leader, Letha Scanzoni, co-author of an evangelical feminist book, *All We're Meant to Be*, used Ephesians 5 to support her idea of egalitarian marriage, claiming mutual submission to be Paul's point there, thus divesting the analogy of its sense.

One of the planks of the feminist platform is that sexual distinctions beyond the biological ones are all culturally defined. Our ideas of femininity, they say, are purely conditioned. If we try giving dump trucks to little girls and tea sets to little boys, things would be quickly reversed, we are told. The only reason no woman has ever been a Grand Master in chess is that women are not socially conditioned to be great chess players. Sounds believable until you think of Russia, the country from which most Grand Masters have come, and a country in which as many women as men play chess (but we would not dare to suggest that the feminine intellect is in any way different from—not to say inferior to—the masculine). Women are not encouraged to seek positions which require aggression, it is said, and therefore aggression is considered a masculine trait. Society can change all this. Just start interchanging roles, encouraging girls to be plant foremen, boys to be nurses. Insist on husbands doing housework and wives taking equal financial responsibility. Make women pay alimony, conscript them for active military service, let men knit and cry in public if they want to, and we'll see what happens.

But all this sort of thing is quite beside the point. The idea of male and female was God's idea. None of us would have thought of it, and God has never defined it for anybody. He's told us what he did—he created them in his own image, male and female—and he's shown us how he did it. He made the man from the dust of the ground and breathed into him the breath of life; then, because he saw in his creation the first thing that was "not good," namely a man alone, he made for the man a woman. He made her *for* the man. To me this is the first constituent of femininity. Then he made her *from* the man—derived, flesh of his flesh, bone of his bone, like and yet wondrously unlike. This is the second constituent. Finally, he brought her to the man, designed exactly to suit his peculiar need, prepared to meet that need for a helper, and then, in divine wisdom and love, given. This is the third constituent.

But what is this man, what is this woman? What are these elusive and indefinable but universally acknowledged qualities on which every culture and society has shaped its existence? The question which feminists resolutely refuse to confront at all is one vastly prior to the question of social conditioning. It is this: *Why* has every society since the beginning of time conditioned its males and females so distinctively? Granted, the ideas of masculinity and femininity have been expressed differently from time to time and from place to place, but the distinctions have without exception been, until the late twentieth century, *preserved*.

Michael Marshall in his profound little book *Gospel Healing and Salvation* says, "Modern man is hung up on his identity with others in lengthy counselings. The Christian realizes that his true identity is a mystery known only to God, and that any attempt at this stage on the road of discipleship to define himself is bound to be blasphemous and destructive of that mysterious work of God forming Christ in him by the power of the Holy Spirit. Certainly the Christian does not define his identity by his actions: that is the very ultimate in anti-Christ, for it is in effect saying that I am my own creator."

Feminists, regrettably, ask us to define ourselves not

as men and women but as "human beings" (whatever that means), identified only by our function in society. We must rid ourselves, Virginia Mollenkott declared at the Washington caucus, of "all gender-based categories."

Through the centuries the church has seen the soul as "female before God"—that is, the receptor, the one who responds, who is created for the other, the one acted upon, the one who gives herself. The structure of the female body, designed to carry, to bear and to nurture—surely it is but the material evidence of the mystery of femininity, a physical sign of metaphysical realities with which we tamper only to our own peril. Femininity is indisputably bound up with the concept of motherhood. This is not social conditioning. It is not a lamentable prejudice of which we ought to try to purify ourselves. It is most certainly not, as some feminists cry, "barbaric." The physical signs, far from being extraneous frills we would do well to ignore or overcome, point to the invisible truth of womanhood, exemplified for all women forever in that simple peasant girl, the virgin Mary, utterly feminine, utterly ready to give herself up to the overshadowing Holy Ghost in the will of God, ready to receive, to bear, to nurture "that holy thing," the Lord Christ, ready to go down into death to give him life, ready to have even her own soul pierced by a sword.

This is an example, I say, for all women forever—not only for those who are the actual mothers of children, but for all who seriously contemplate the Creation Story and accept their place as it is described there, not a competitive one, not even (heaven forbid) an "equal" one, but a different one, mysterious, defined at last only by God the Creator himself, with its own divinely designed kingdom, its own power, its own glory, and all in perfect complement to that other mystery which every real woman recognizes when she sees it—recognizes but cannot define: masculinity.

A Mother's Testament

While I was writing a letter at my desk fifteen years ago my small daughter interrupted to say that she had dropped two sucres (Ecuadorian coins) into the rain barrel, and could she please put on her bathing suit and swim to the bottom to get them? I said she could.

Today she is twenty-one. She is a thousand miles from home and when I called at 6:45 A.M. to wish her a happy birthday I caught her munching a prune and an almond, the prelude to a breakfast of hot cracked wheat cereal, brewer's yeast drink, toast and grapefruit. (She's an even more fanatical food freak than her mother.) She chatted happily about the blue outfit I'd sent her, about the papers she must write before graduation, which is only three weeks away, and about her wedding, which is nine weeks away.

A mother may, I suppose, be forgiven for pausing to remember these twenty-one swift years. When she was born she was a marvel and an object of deep concern to the Indians of the jungle where we lived, for she was put not only in a bed separate from that of her parents, but even in a separate room. Demons, the Indians warned us anxiously, would certainly "lick" her if she was not protected between her father and mother. When we assured them that no demon would bother her at all, they shook their heads in bewilderment: another of the inexplicable differences between themselves and these foreigners. Demons don't like foreign children. But what about vampires? That, we knew, would have been a real danger if we had not lived in a screened house.

She was carried around in an *aparinga*, an Indian carrying cloth, not only by her mother but by Indian women and girls who asked if they might "borrow" her for a little while. She learned two languages at once and managed to keep them separate in her mind. She played, swam, walked the trails and ate fish heads with the Indian kids. The "slumber parties" she went to were in Indian houses where she took her blanket and curled up on the bamboo slats beside her friends, coming home in the morning to announce that breakfast had been soup. "What kind of soup?" I once asked. "Oh, rat soup, I guess," she said, and she was right.

Because she always went barefoot she had to wash her feet every night before going to bed, a chore she sometimes wished she could get out of. One evening while washing the supper dishes in the river she looked up to see a beautiful sunset. "It looks as though Jesus might come through there," she said to me, "and then I wouldn't even have to wash my feet. Jesus would wash my feet for me—he's kind."

In a small notebook I kept the accounts Val sometimes dictated to me of her doings with the Indians. One fragment from the notebook reads:

"We got to a little pool, a little lake. Uba just got one fish with her hands. With a knife she whacked it. And then we went to get *pitumu* [palm fruit]. We got *chicha* [manioc drink] where the little lake was. It was Ipa's *chicha*. She squeezed it for me into a little leaf, because we didn't have any cups. At home we have cups. I was thirsty. Kumi, Kinta and I drank some. The rest didn't have any because there wasn't any left. Then we got the *pitumu* and made a basket with some leaves, and then we came home. I saw wild pig and tapir footprints and that's all."

Later: "I took some poison down to the river and watched how Ana fixed it. Then I got some and put it in a little hole in the ground and punched it and punched it and punched it, and when the leaves got soft I put it in the basket and then in the water. Soon I got a little fish, a little fish, and a little fish [this is the Indian way of saying 'three fish']. Their names were *kuniwae, niwimu* and *arakawae*. I brought them to Gimari's fire and put them on a little stick that was burning and they got toasted and then I ate them. And that's all."

One evening I overheard Valerie singing to her kitten:

Amazing grace, how sweet the sound
That saved a wretch like you.

Among the questions asked on a single day were, "Why can't we breathe under water?" "Will we go through a rainbow when we go to God's house?" "Owls got kinda paper faces, don't they?" "Can God make the tea stop coming out of the pot?" and "Why do dogs have knees in the back of their legs?"

Hers was a happy life with the Indians, but she dreamed of having a brother or sister. Standing in front of a mirror once she said, "I sometimes think this is my sister, my twin, and I talk to her and she answers me and smiles."

Perhaps this solitude helped her to understand the solitude of others. She loved taking care of things. In the jungle, making people comfortable meant, among other things, building a fire, and she spent a good deal of time at this. I found her tending two tiny fires underneath our house (which was on stilts), "one for me," she explained, "and one for my little birdie so he won't be cold." She had put the baby woodpecker's basket close by. Another time she was tucking up her small friend Taemaenta (both were about five years old) in her hammock, covering him with a doll blanket and fanning up the fire. When she climbed in beside him I inquired what she was up to. "Just being kind to Taemaenta because his mother is gone," she said. She carried her own dolls around in an *aparinga*, covering their heads with a rag when the trail led out into the sunshine, protecting them with her hand when she stooped to go under a fallen tree or through a patch of underbrush.

Her education for the first three years was the Calvert School correspondence course, begun under taxing conditions since we had no place to put books and things, living, as we were then, in a wall-less house. It was difficult to concentrate with Indians hanging over her shoulder, peering at the pictures, fingering the books, trying out the crayons, snipping things with the scissors.

The third-grade work included a lesson on mythology. As I was telling the story of Pandora's box I tried to explain the meaning of hope. After giving several other illustrations I asked, "What was my hope when your daddy died?" "Me!" was the immediate reply.

She was indeed. In the bleakest times she was there, a gift of joy, lifting her little face in love, smiling, not knowing anything of the need she met.

She thought much about God and heaven (which was to her not only the Father's house but her daddy's as well). I sometimes wrote down her prayers after I had kissed her goodnight. I did this not because I feared they would otherwise be lost (the great angel with the golden censer will see that they are not lost) but because I knew that they would be lost to me. I would forget. And also because I had no one, at that time, to tell them to.

"Dear Lord, thank you for this sentence: 'There is a green hill far away where the dear, dear Lord Jesus was crucified.' Jesus, you know that we don't understand your words. Just like those people long ago, when you told them you were going to come alive. They didn't understand. We're just like those people. So help us to understand. Help us not to lie and disobey and steal. Let's be sweet. And help me with my arithmetic tomorrow. In Jesus' name. Amen." She was eight years old.

She had seen birth and suffering and death in our life with the Indians, had acquired a "nerve of knowledge" that rendered her sensitive. When I asked if she ever thought about death she said, "Yes, sometimes when I'm washing my feet. You know how the sink is dry, and the water creeps up the sides when I'm filling it? There are little points around the edges of the water, and I think these points are the number of days before I'm going to die, and go to see my daddy. But I don't count them. I splash the water up quickly." With these intimations of mortality she was at the same time full of joy. She told me several times of dreams in which she found herself floating and singing. If she wakened in the night, she often sang. A friend described her walk as "not on but slightly above the ground."

When she was twelve I went into her room one evening to thank her for washing all the dishes when I had guests. "Mommy!" she said as I started to leave. "I want to thank *you* for my *whole life*! For all you've given me and for all the things you've done for me and for all the food you've cooked for me!"

To look at the woman who was that child of nine years ago and to realize that I am thanked for what I cooked and did and gave—*thanked* for doing what I could not possibly have helped wanting with all my heart to do—is to understand in a new light the words of Jesus, "It is more blessed to give than to receive." More "blessed"? He must have meant that it is a happier thing to *aim at the giving* rather than at the receiving, but, strangely, if we put the giving first the receiving necessarily follows. For me, from this child, the receiving seems to have been without interruption. It is not immediately so for all, I know. If we give out of love, however, there is ultimately no way in heaven or earth to avoid receiving, and receiving far more than we could possibly give.

Nine more weeks. Shall we have a multi-media presentation flashed on the walls of the church as she moves down the aisle? Swimming to the bottom of the rain barrel, eating rat soup, drinking *chicha* from a leaf cup, snuggling with Taemaenta in her hammock, floating and singing? Not a very workable idea. But I shall be remembering, and giving thanks.

As We Forgive Those . . . .

A young minister leading a Bible study recently cited a reference in the Psalms to sin.

"I don't care what you say!" a middle-aged woman blurted out. "I'm not going to forgive my mother-in-law! What she did to me I could never forgive."

The minister had not mentioned forgiveness, or any specific sin, but the Word of God, sharper than any two-edged sword, had pierced the woman's heart. Her outburst was a dead giveaway of the resentment that smoldered beneath the surface.

A girl I'll call Sandra phoned several months ago to tell me that she had just been asked to be godmother to her friend Vicky's child. It was impossible, Sandra said, to consider such a thing since Vicky, once a close friend, had hurt her very deeply. The two couples had vacationed together and their friendship disintegrated over a series of trivial but unforgivable hurts. They had hardly seen each other since, and now here was Vicky expecting Sandra to be her child's godmother. What was Sandra to do?

"Forgive her," I said.

"Forgive her! But she isn't even sorry. I don't think she even remembers how she hurt me!"

Nevertheless, I told her, if it was her Christian duty she was asking me about, there was no question as to what it was.

"You mean I'm the one who has to make the move?"

"Do you expect God to forgive you for your sins?"

"Well, certainly."

"Then you must forgive Vicky."

"Is there someplace in the Bible that actually *says* that?"

"Remember the Lord's Prayer? 'Forgive us our trespasses as we forgive those who trespass against us.' That's followed by a pretty plain statement: 'If you do not forgive men their trespasses, neither will your Father forgive you your trespasses.' "

I could almost hear Sandra catch her breath on the telephone. There was a pause.

"I never thought of that. And I said that prayer just this morning. So . . . I can't expect to be forgiven unless I forgive?"

She didn't see how she could do that. I agreed most emphatically that she could not—not without God's grace. Everything in human nature goes against that idea. But the gospel is the message of *reconciliation*. Reconciliation not only to God, but to his purposes in the world, and to all our fellow human beings. We talked for a little while about the absolute necessity of forgiveness. It is a command. It is the road to restoration of ruptured friendships. It releases us from ourselves. I promised

Sandra I would pray for the grace of God to work in her and in Vicky, and that she would be enabled freely and completely to forgive.

"But what if she still isn't sorry?"

"We don't pray, 'Forgive us our trespasses as we forgive those who ask us to.' We say 'as we forgive those who trespass against us.' It's not a matter of *ignoring* what's been done. When God forgives he doesn't merely overlook our trespasses. He doesn't ask us to overlook others' trespasses either—he asks us to forgive them. So that means our Christian obligation is to forgive anybody who has invaded our rights, our territory, our comfort, our self-image, whether they acknowledge the invasion or not."

A week later I learned that Sandra's and my prayers had been answered far beyond what either of us had had faith to expect. Not only did Sandra forgive, but Vicky even apologized, and the two were reconciled.

To forgive is to die. It is to give up one's right to self, which is precisely what Jesus requires of anyone who wants to be his disciple.

"If anyone wants to follow in my footsteps, he must give up all right to himself, carry his cross every day and keep close behind me. For the man who wants to save his life will lose it, but the man who loses his life for my sake will save it."

Following Christ means walking the road he walked, and in order to forgive us he had to die. His follower may not refuse to relinquish his own right, his own territory, his own comfort, or anything that he regards as his. Forgiveness is relinquishment. It is a laying down. No one can take it from us, any more than anyone could take the life of Jesus if he had not laid it down of his own will. But we can do as he did. We can offer it up, writing off whatever loss it may entail, in the sure knowledge that the man who loses his life or his reputation or his "face" or anything else for the sake of Christ will save it.

The woman who hates her mother-in-law is wallowing in offenses. Her resentment has grown and festered over twenty-seven years, and it is "fierce in proportion as it is futile," as John Oman wrote. Her bitterness, the minister tells me, has poisoned her own life and that of the church of which she is a member.

The Bible tells a story about a man who, being forgiven by the king a debt of millions of pounds, went immediately to one who owed him a few shillings, grabbed him by the throat and demanded payment. We react to a story like that. "Nobody acts like that!" we say, and then, grabbed, as it were, by the truth of the story ourselves, we realize, "Nobody but us!"

When Jesus, nailed to a Roman cross, prayed, "Father, forgive them," he wielded a weapon against which Caesar himself had no power. The helpless, dying Son of God, a picture of defeat, proclaimed the victory of Inexorable Love. Who can stand up to the force of forgiveness?

Several times people have come to me to confess bitterness which they have felt toward me about which I had known nothing at all. They knew I had known nothing. Were they then taking occasion to air a grievance which ought to have been a matter between them and God? Was this a pious method of expressing sinful feelings which they should have asked God to cleanse? The Bible does not tell us to go to one against whom we have a grievance. It tells us to go to one who has a grievance against us: "If you are offering your gift at the altar, and there remember that your brother has something against you, leave your gift there before the altar and go; first be reconciled to your brother, and then come and offer your gift" (Matthew 5:23-24). We are commanded to forgive anyone who has trespassed. We are not told to call his attention to the offense. We are to ask the forgiveness of anyone against whom we have trespassed. This may be a long journey for us, geographically or emotionally and spiritually. But if we mean to be disciples of the Crucified we must make that journey and slay the dragon of self-interest. We thereby align ourselves with God, acting no longer independently of him or for our own "rights."

Those who bear the Cross must also bear others' burdens. This includes the burden of responsibility for sin as well as the sharing of suffering. What room can there possibly be for touchiness or a self-regarding fastidiousness in the true burden-bearer? Forgiveness is a clear-eyed and cool-headed acceptance of the burden of responsibility.

The life of St. Francis of Assisi exemplified his own profound understanding that "it is in pardoning that we are pardoned."

If we too intend to take up the Cross we commit

ourselves to the same quality of life. Then we can with truthfulness sing

> *I take, O Cross, thy shadow for my abiding place.*
> *I ask no other sunshine than the sunshine of thy*
>   *face,*
> *Content to let the world go by, to know no gain or*
>   *loss,*
> *My sinful self, my only shame; my glory all the*
>   *Cross.*

One Difference Between Me and Sparrows

I have, for this month, a very quiet room in the top of a very quiet old house on a quiet hillside in New Hampshire. No sound disturbs my thoughts except that of white-throated sparrows, black-capped chickadees, crickets and some horses who tear quietly at the long grass around the house and occasionally puff or mutter under their breath. My mother is the only other resident, and she is quieter than the sparrows and the rest. She fixes my breakfast and afterward, when I start to carry dishes to the kitchen, she says, "Run along. I'll do these. You get to your writing."

There is only one thing wrong with a situation like this. If what you write turns out to be bilge, you haven't a rag of excuse. You can't tell anybody that it was because you couldn't concentrate. It wasn't because you had so many other responsibilities and unavoidable interruptions. It wasn't because of "the pace of modern life." It was because . . . well, admit it, it was because a lot of what's inside is bilge, God help us all.

The Bible says the just shall live by faith. The "just" is not a special category of specially gifted or inspired saints. It is the people whose hearts are turned toward God. The people who know that their own righteousness doesn't count for much and who therefore have accepted God's. I belong in that category. Therefore the rule for me is the rule for all the rest: live by faith. So I have been pondering, up here in this quiet room, what it means for a writer to live by faith. It was easy enough to come up with some things it doesn't mean. It does not mean that my intellect need not be hard at work. It does not mean that I trust God to do my work for me, any more than for a housewife to live by faith means she expects God to do her dishes or make her beds. It does not mean that I have a corner on inspiration that Norman Mailer, say, or Truman Capote don't claim. (I don't know whether Mr. Mailer or Mr. Capote live by faith—I haven't come across any comments by either on the subject.)

The great prophets of the Old Testament lived by faith, but they were certainly divinely inspired. Does this mean that God alone—and not they, too—was responsible for the work they did? Even though they were acted upon in a special sense by the Spirit of God as I don't ever expect to be acted upon, they had to pay a price. Each of them had to make the individual commitment when he was called, and to offer up then and there his own plans and hopes (and surely his reputation) in order that his personality, his temperament, his intellect, his peculiar gifts and experience might be the instruments through which the Spirit did his work, or the console upon which he played. All this, even though I am no prophet, I must take seriously.

But there is one other thing that living by faith does not mean. This is the thing that makes me furrow my brow and sigh, because I can't help wishing that it did mean this. If in fact I have sided with the "just," if I am willing to work as hard as I can, if I arrange things physically to contribute to the highest concentration and if I discipline myself to sit down at the typewriter for X number of hours per day (even when the fresh perfume of the balsams comes through the windows, calling me to the woods; even when the lake glitters in the sunshine and says, "Come on!"), may I then expect that what I turn out will stop the world, bring the public panting to the bookstores, shine as the brightness of the firmament?

I may not. There are no promises to cover anything of the kind.

In an Isak Dinesen story a lady asked a cardinal, "Are you sure that it is God whom you serve?" The cardinal sighed deeply. "That, madam," he replied, "is a risk that the artists and priests of the world must take."

And if they take the risk, they stake their lives on the task and it may turn out to be no more effective than Moses' efforts with Pharaoh, or the words of the prophets to the people to whom they cried. I get this far in my argument with myself and am brought up short with the realization that I cannot take comfort from that, for in the case of Moses and the prophets there was nothing wrong with either the messenger or the message. In my case, there is a lot wrong with both.

Then I think of Abel. And here's comfort. Abel's name is listed in the Hall of Fame of Hebrews 11. Like the others in that list (and a motley assortment it is), he is there for one thing, and only one thing: the exercise of faith. The demonstration of his faith was his offering. The thing that made his offering acceptable while Cain's was unacceptable was faith. Faith did not guarantee the "success" of the sacrifice. In human terms it was no help at all. Abel ended up dead as a result of it. But the manner in which he offered his gift—"by faith"—made it, the Bible says, "a more excellent sacrifice" than Cain's, and qualified him for the roster of Hebrews.

For me, then, for whom writing happens to be the task, living by faith means several things.

It means accepting the task from God (taking the "risk" here that the cardinal spoke of). Here is a thing to be done. It appears to be a thing to be done by me, so I'll do it, and I'll do it *for God.*

It means coming at the task trustingly. That's the way Abel brought his sacrifice, I'm sure. Not with fear, not with a false humility that it wasn't "good enough." What would ever be good enough, when it comes right down to it? "All things come of Thee, O Lord, and of Thine own have we given Thee." All that distinguishes one thing from another is the manner of its offering. I must remember that the God to whom I bring it has promised to receive. That's all I need to know.

It means doing the job with courage to face the consequences. I might, of course, write a best-seller. Most of us feel we could handle that kind of consequence. (God knows we couldn't, and doesn't suffer us to be tempted above that we are able.) On the other hand, I might fail. Abel was murdered. Jeremiah was dropped into a pit of slime. John the Baptist got his head chopped off. These were much worse fates than being delivered into the hands of one's literary critics. ("Much worse?" one of my selves says, and "Oh, come now—much worse," answers another. "Come off it. You're not putting yourself in a class with those towering figures, are you?" "I guess I was for a minute there.") Is the faith that gives me the courage I need based on former literary success? Not for a moment. For each time I sit down to begin a new book I'm aware that I may have shot my wad. It's another kind of faith I need, faith *in God*.

It means giving it everything I've got. Now I have to acknowledge that I've never done this. I've never finished any job in my life and been able to survey it proudly and say, "Look at that! I certainly did my best that time!" I look at the job and say, "Why didn't I do such and such? This really ought to be done over." But "giving it everything I've got" is my goal. I cannot claim to be living by faith unless I'm living in obedience. Even the miracles Jesus performed were contingent on somebody's obedience, on somebody's doing some little thing such as filling up water pots, stretching out a hand, giving up a lunch. The work I do needs to be transformed. I know that very well. But there has to be something there to *be* transformed. It's my responsibility to see that it's there.

I can hear the white-throated sparrow now. Sending out his pure sweet call, filling the air from his tiny syrinx with the song he was made to sing, an offering "good and acceptable and perfect" to his Maker—a fact which, unless the sparrow is equipped to doubt, he need never struggle to believe.

Like the sparrow, I've got a song to sing. Unlike the sparrow, I must sing mine by faith.

The Trail to Shandia

There is a road east of the Andes from the little tea-growing town of Puyo, to an unnamed point in the jungle just beyond the mostly Indian town of Pano. When I lived in Ecuador most of the road was not there at all, and it would have taken you three days to cover that distance. I covered it a few weeks ago in the space of a few hours in a jeep driven by a missionary named Ella Rae. We traveled along the south side of the Ansuc River and crossed, on a suspension bridge, the Atun Yacu, which we once crossed by dugout canoe. The road took us through the towns of Napo and Tena and then straight up the middle of what used to be a mission station airstrip in Pano. When the road ended at the Pano River, Ella Rae bade us good-bye and we set out on foot for Shandia, one of the places where I used to live. I had been over the trail from Tena to Shandia many times, but, although the government has laid logs cross-wise to make walking easier, horses and cows have been making use of it and the trail was in the worst condition I'd ever seen.

We were two women and one man—he in shorts and rubber knee boots, we in standard jungle garb of blouses, skirts and tennis shoes. As we plowed our way through the mud some spiritual parallels came to mind.

Every step of faith is a step of *faith*. In some places the logs were submerged in mud. Finding one to put your foot on did not make it easier to find the next one.

Each step was a *decision*, but to make it a *problem* would have halted progress altogether. Sometimes the choice was to balance on a three-inch-in-diameter log laid parallel to the path and take the chance of slipping off sideways and falling into the mud, or to step deliberately into mud (which was like peanut butter) up to one's knees, or to try to beat one's way through the tangle at the side of the trail (and of course that tangle could always hold snakes). You had to keep moving. Decisions, therefore, had to be snap decisions. If we had let each step be a problem, to be paused and pondered over, we'd still be there. If a decision turned out to be the wrong one, which it often seemed to be, you simply pulled yourself out and kept on.

The trail—always leading us to our goal—took on varied aspects. We were not always in mud up to our knees, or trying to find a footing on logs which were in some places floating and in some places submerged. For short spaces the trail was of gravel. Sometimes there were hills to climb and rivers to wade through where we got the chance to rinse off a few pounds of accumulated jungle soil. At times we were in sunshine where the forest had been cut back to make pasture, at other times in deep shade.

There was a tiny footprint in front of me. You learn when you travel jungle trails to recognize the differences in footprints. A party of Indians had evidently preceded us not long before. One of them was a child no more than three. As we came to what seemed to me impassable sections, I found myself spurred on by the knowledge that where the trail was firmer I would find the little footprint. Sure enough. That little person had made it through what was for him hip-high mud, across the precarious logs, into the streams, up the hills and down the slick ravines. There is something amazingly heartening in the knowledge that somebody else has been over the course before—especially if it's somebody who has had manifestly greater difficulties than ours to overcome. Most of the time there was no evidence at all of his going, and I could lose heart. But here and there again the evidence lay, clear and unmistakable. If he had made it, so could I.

We made it. We reached the house my husband Jim Elliot had built twenty-three years ago. The only reason it still stands is that it was built on a cement slab with poured cement walls up to the level of the window sills, boards from there up to the aluminum roof. An ordinary jungle house would have vanished long since. Mary began sweeping out the bat droppings and the dead cockroaches and spiders, tidying up, lighting candles and cooking a simple supper while Frank and I went to visit the Indians in their houses nearby. Thirteen years lay lightly on most of them, but a generation of children had become unrecognizable.

We pulled out some bedding I had left stored in steel

drums and stayed the night in the house. A mouse had to be evicted from one of the mattresses. The sound of the Atun Yacu at the foot of the cliff was the same as it had always been. The shadows cast by the candles seemed to take the shapes familiar to me from the nights when I had risen to feed my baby in this very bedroom. Her toy wicker furniture was still there, its upholstery mildewed and nearly colorless.

Not quite three weeks have passed, and I sit in my green-carpeted study in Massachusetts. The trail—always leading to the goal—does take on different aspects. Soon I will face my seminary students again to remind them that each footstep along the trail matters, not only the goal toward which they aspire. The clean, hard gravel matters, but so does the slough with the floating logs, the hill and the deep ravine. The traveler who makes each decision about where to put his foot is not different from the person who has reached the house and rests at last by the fireplace with a cup of tea and a candle. Are they prospective ministers? Then they must be now, while they are on the jouney, true men and women, attending to today's task, living their lives today. They do not see into heaven. They have to live on earth. They must move steadily, putting one foot in front of the other, no matter whether it is the log, the rock or the mire that receives it. They must rightly discharge each small duty, whether it be to a professor, a landlady, a wife or an employer.

I will remind them, too, that the Bible does not speak of problems. As Corrie ten Boom says, "God has no problems, only plans." We ought to think not of problems but of purpose. We encounter the obstacle, we make a choice—always with the goal in mind.

We are conditioned nowadays, however, to define everything as a problem. A little girl on a TV commercial pipes, "I have this terrible *problem* with my hair! But my mommy bought No More Tangles, and now there's no more tangles!" A group of young wives asked me to speak to them on "The Problems of Widowhood." I declined, explaining in the first place that I did not regard widowhood as a problem, and in the second place that if I did I was not sure I had any warrant for unloading my own problems onto the shoulders of young women who had enough of their own, and in the third place a widow has only one "problem," when it comes right down to it—she has no husband. And that's something nobody can do anything about.

Life is full of things we can't do anything about, but which we are supposed to do something with. "He himself endured a cross and thought nothing of its shame because of the joy." A very different story from the one which would have been written if Jesus had been prompted by the spirit of our own age: "Don't just endure the cross—*think* about it, talk about it, share it, express your gut-level feelings, get in touch with yourself, find out who you are, define the problem, analyze it, get counseling, get the experts' opinions, discuss solutions, work through it." Jesus endured. He thought *nothing* of the shame. The freedom, the freshness of that valiant selflessness is like a strong wind. How badly such a wind is needed to sweep away the pollution of our self-preoccupation!

Analysis can make you feel guilty for being human. To be human, of course, means to be sinful, and for our sinfulness we must certainly "feel" the guilt which is rightly ours—but not everything human is sinful. There is a man on the radio every afternoon from California whose consummate arrogance in making an instant analysis of every caller's difficulties is simply breathtaking. A woman called in to talk about her problems with her husband who happens to be an actor. "Oh," said the counselor, "of course the only reason anybody goes into acting is because they need approval." Bang. Husband's problem identified. Next question. I turned off the radio and asked myself, with rising guilt feelings, "Do I need approval?" Answer: yes. Does anybody not need approval? Is there anybody who is content to live his life without so much as a nod from anybody else? Wouldn't he be, of all men, the most devilishly self-centered? Wouldn't his supreme solitude be the most hellish? It's human to want to know that you please somebody.

We visited another place where I lived—Tewaenon—where the Aucas live. It had been sixteen years since I had seen them, but they remembered me, calling me by the name they had given me, "Gikari," and everybody beginning at once, as was their custom, to tell me what they had done since they saw me. Dabu, with two of his three wives, came walking up the airstrip and began immediately—there are no greetings in Auca—to tell me that when he had heard of the death of my second husband he had cried. This prompted Ipa to remark that she had sat down and written me a letter when she heard of his death, but on rereading the letter said to herself, "It's no good," and threw it away. Sometimes readers of things that I write tell me long afterward that they have thought of writing me a letter, or have written one and discarded it, thinking, "She doesn't need my approval." Well, they're mistaken—for wouldn't it be a lovely thing to know that a footprint you have left on the trail has, just by being there, heartened somebody else?

All Creatures Here Below

The *New Yorker* had a picture on its cover in February 1968 of a group of people looking at sleeping puppies in a pet shop window. Every face was alight, and the women, of course, were tapping on the glass, trying to elicit some response from the fetching little beagles in the pen.

What is it we see in the faces of puppies? What else in the whole world instantly softens the expressions of the hardest people as does the sight of a little puppy trotting gaily along the sidewalk? Is there something eternal, some intimation of unutterable sweetness there which we know will be gone in a matter of weeks? We want to get our hands on the softness; we crave response. People who would not dream of addressing a stranger on the street will address a puppy and then often, as though they cannot help themselves, the owner of the puppy as well.

Some years ago my husband and I bought a tiny purebred Scottish terrier. He had a box-shaped body on which black fur grew in the shape of a horse blanket, shaggy and shiny. He had another smaller box for a head, with jaunty chin whiskers, wonderfully bright black eyes and a glistening black nose. His ears pointed sharply, and he moved them up, sideways and back—he could even revolve them—depending on whether he was looking, listening or waiting hopefully to be petted. His tail was a little cone in almost constant motion. His feet were like short flanges at the ends of his unbelievably short legs. His legs were, in fact, just barely long enough to keep his chin off the floor.

The dog's name was MacPhearce. He had a terrier's feistiness and could bark sharply or growl like a tenor gargling, but was putting on an act ("Is he trained to kill on command?" a man on the street asked), for he was really very affectionate and badly wanted friends.

I put a blue collar on him and took him out on a blue leash. (He did not, however, wear a plaid coat or rubbers. It seemed logical to me that the coat he came with was designed for his needs.) People would catch a glimpse of him and stop in their tracks. "Look at this dog!" they would say, if they had anyone with them to say it to, or, "Isn't he adorable?" they would say to me. People under forty often said, "What kind of dog is that?" and people over forty said, "Oh, a Scotty! You don't see many of them anymore!" MacPhearce was not aware that he had gone out of style. He had been succeeded by Boston terriers, then by poodles and boxers and Lhasa apsos. But it never bothered him much, and he behaved as though he was exactly what he was meant to be, which is more than can be said of some human beings. One said, "Ooohhh—I can't stand it, he's so cute!"

I wonder if God felt anything like that on the day he created such creatures. "It is very good" is what he is reported to have said, and I suppose we cannot expect the Almighty to have been thrilled, or even impressed. It was exactly what he had meant. The animal was the living proof of the divine idea.

MacPhearce was not a sinner, theologically speaking, and therefore fulfilled God's intention for him every moment of his life. My husband wrote years ago about a dog he had named Lassie. He believed that she had been "assigned" to him. It was her business to keep him happy, and perhaps of all the marvelous things dogs do for man (herding sheep, retrieving birds, pulling sleds, leading the blind, rescuing the freezing or the drowning), none is more marvelous than this: they are comforters and companions. They think always of their master. What is he doing? Can I accompany him? Is he happy? How can I cheer him?

A woman I know found her teen-age daughter lying on the living room rug one evening, sobbing into the curly fur of their cocker spaniel. The mother had on many occasions wondered if the dog was worth all the fuss and trouble of training, feeding, cleaning fur off the rugs and furniture. She stopped wondering when she saw that the dog was a refuge and a friend to the child when she would have found it impossible to cry on anyone's shoulder. The mother made up her mind then and there that as long as she had children, at least, she would have a dog. (She has since decided that even she needs him.)

My old friend Dorothy who lives on the Cape has had dachshunds, terriers, poodles and a Scotty. "Oh my, they give so much," she says, "and they ask so little!"

C. S. Lewis had some lovely things to say about animals in his *Letters to an American Lady.* "I will never laugh at anyone for grieving over a loved beast. I think God wants us to love him *more*, not to love creatures (even animals) *less*. No person, animal, flower, or even pebble, has ever been loved too much—i.e., more than every one of God's works deserves."

In another letter he wrote, "We were talking about cats and dogs the other day and decided that both have consciences but the dog, being an honest, humble person, always has a bad one, but the cat is a Pharisee and always has a good one. When he sits and stares you out of countenance he is thanking God that he is not as these dogs, or these humans, or even as these other cats!"

A dog can gaze with adoration and not be embarrassed, but if he finds himself gazed at by a group not entirely sympathetic, he seems to know this and will often busy himself with licking a paw, or will perhaps decide that he has business elsewhere. He accepts himself for what he is, and us human beings for whatever we may be, and thus teaches us a lesson in the grace of acceptance. Dogs can adapt themselves to whatever treatment we may dish out. If we step on a tail by accident its owner may yelp but will be wagging it at once in forgiveness. A dog's eyes may be filled with reproach if we have left him alone too long, if we go out in the car and tell him to stay, or if his dinner is late, but the reproach is gentle and loving, and he will come and lay his head in our lap seventy times seven.

A truck went by the house the other day labeled *Old Mother Hubbard Oven-Baked Dog Foods and Laboratory Diets*. The pet food business is an enormous and lucrative one. Any pet shop displays a staggering variety of feeding dishes, foods, toys, medicines, shampoos, flea soaps and powders, beds, baskets, carrying cases, cages, leashes, collars—some of them rhinestone-studded—and garments, including galoshes and raincoats for poodles. We insult our pets by not allowing them to be animals. We violate their being when we try to make them human.

"Love the pride of your dogs," wrote Isak Dinesen. "Let them not grow fat." Put not on them outrageous frippery, I would add. Pamper them not with furniture and food luxurious for people but indecent for animals. Recognize what they are, love them for that, let them love you because you love them for what they are and not because you have made of them a poor facsimile of yourself.

George MacDonald, the Scottish preacher and novelist of the nineteenth century, believed that "dogs always behold the face of the Father." To study a dog's face will make you wonder about the redemption of all creation. Do dogs have souls? We have no clue to that in Scripture. We are told, however, that "everything that exists in heaven or earth shall find its perfection and fulfillment in Christ."

A lady once asked Dr. Harry Ironside of Moody Church in Chicago about the salvation of dogs. She was heartbroken over the death of her little white dog, and was not sure she would be able to enjoy heaven at all if he was not going to be there. "Madam," replied Dr. Ironside, "if when you get to heaven you want your little white dog, I can assure you that he will be there."

What the "perfection and fulfillment" of little white dogs or little black puppies named MacPhearce may mean is not, for us at any rate, a very important question. But it may remind us of unspeakably important questions. Responsibility to our Creator. Obedience to his call. Fulfillment of his purpose for us as men and women who have been given the mandate to take care of the earth. Then we can join with all creatures great and small, and even with the stars of the firmament of which Joseph Addison wrote in 1712:

> *In reason's ear they all rejoice and utter forth a glorious voice:*
> *Forever singing as they shine, "The hand that made us is divine."*

Five Kids and Peace

The house was large, white, set well back from the street, and surrounded with lawns, gardens and beautiful big trees—the sort of place that could easily keep a full-time gardener busy. It was nearly suppertime of an autumn afternoon, and as my hostess, who had met me at the airport, took me through the side door and into the kitchen, I could smell beef stew and wood smoke, just the sort of things I wanted to smell in a place like that. We went through a large hall with a beautiful staircase and into a small sitting room where a fire burned and three boys were sprawled prone on the floor, two of them playing a game, one reading.

"Boys, I want you to meet Mrs. Leitch."

All three were on their feet at once, coming toward me to shake hands. Not only were they not reluctant or surly, they acted as though they were sincerely glad to see me.

After I was shown my room I joined Arlita, my hostess, in the kitchen to help with supper. She set about making biscuits while I cut up apples for Waldorf salad. A few minutes before supper was ready a couple of the boys appeared and in no time had set the table, poured the milk, carried in the food.

The dining room had an elegant fireplace and mantelpiece, a bay window filled with plants, and an enormous round cherry table. Joe, who is a doctor, sat opposite the fireplace with his wife at his side. I sat across from them and between us the four sons and one daughter, ages nine to sixteen. We all clasped hands for grace. Conversation ranged from schoolwork, the church, the neighbors, the old house a few blocks away where I used to live, to mathematics and the meaning of a passage of Scripture. All participated. All also took it upon themselves to see to the comfort of their guest, passing me the biscuits, the jam, the salt, asking if I'd have another bowl of stew, filling my water glass. It seemed that each child understood that he was on the entertainment committee. The fact that I was a contemporary of their parents did not absolve them of gracious responsibility. They were even eager to look after me, eager to hear what I had to say.

The dining room doesn't have an observation window with one-way glass to which I can take certain parents I can think of to observe this model family, seated around the cherry table, alert yet relaxed, disciplined yet hilarious, attentive yet at ease. And of course the family would object very strenuously to anyone's holding them up as a model. Yet they are. All families, in the last analysis, are models—of *something*. Some of *cosmos*, that wonderful Greek word which signifies order and arrangement. Some of *chaos*, its opposite—disorder and confusion.

At the end of the meal everybody sang. I can't remember what gospel songs they sang, but I remember the hearty way they all joined. Then Joe read the Bible. They talked about what it meant. The youngest son was asked first to explain what he thought it was all about and was then challenged, corrected and encouraged by siblings and parents. Joe asked for prayer requests and each child thought of somebody he wanted prayed for—a schoolmate who seemed hungry to know God, a Jewish lady whose husband had died, a kid on drugs. When the prayers were finished Joe and Arlita and I went to the sitting room to talk by the fire. All was quiet. I was dimly aware of movement in the other rooms—the table being cleared, dishes washed. Later I heard a piano and a flute. People were practicing, homework was undoubtedly being done, but all of it without strife, without one interruption to the parents who, so far as I noticed, had issued no instructions to anybody when we got up from the table.

Later in the evening I noted the stillness.

"Are the kids in bed?" I asked.

"What time is it?" Arlita said.

"10:45."

"Then they're in bed. Usually we say goodnight to them, but occasionally when we have company they don't come down."

This almost took my breath away. I've visited in a good many homes where the going-to-bed routine takes the better part of the evening, with wheedling, threats, pleas, prolonged negotiations and eventual capitulation.

How, I wanted to know, do you do it? Such order, such peace, such fun as everyone seemed to have, and such smooth running of oiled wheels. I grew up in a family where the same things could have been said, but that was another generation, another day. Walking still occurred to people as a possibility if they had to get somewhere, and it was still acceptable simply to sit on the porch some evenings and not go anywhere. So how, in this day and age, did Joe and Arlita do it?

They looked at each other as though the question had not arisen before. Arlita smiled.

"Well . . . " she hesitated, trying to think how they did do it. "I'm sure we did just what you did. We decided how we wanted it to be and then we did it that way. Isn't that right, Joe?"

"That's right. In fact, we decided before the children were born how we wanted things to be. The going-to-bed business, for example. I don't want to hate my kids, and if I had them in my hair all evening, if I had to fight to get them down and fight to get them up again in the morning, I'd hate them. So after they've reached eight or nine years of age we don't tell them when they have to go to bed. We tell them when they have to be at the breakfast table. We give them each an alarm clock, and if they know they have to be washed, dressed, combed, in their right minds and in their places at 7:30, they soon figure out for themselves when to go to bed and when to get up."

It worked. Next morning, which was Saturday, the children were downstairs to do their appointed tasks. At

7:30 we sat down to sausage, fried apples, scrambled eggs, coffee cake, orange juice and coffee. Arlita had not cooked the breakfast, the kids had. They had organized things so that the whole job was done in a quarter of an hour or so. The table was set, the food on it, hot and appetizing, on time.

Does the system ever break down? I wanted to know. There are lapses, Joe and Arlita said, and privileges sometimes have to be withdrawn, but there's a lot of camaraderie in doing the jobs, and everybody likes to see it work. I had never seen a more beautifully ordered home, and neither had I ever seen a better-adjusted, more likable and outgoing bunch of kids. There must be a connection.

A house the size of theirs needs a lot of maintenance. Nobody comes in to cook, clean or garden. The whole family works. A list of special jobs is posted every so often—woodcutting, window washing, floor waxing, the sort of jobs that aren't done every week—and the children sign up for whatever they're willing to tackle. Then each child makes out a three-by-five card for each job and puts down the time he spent at it. The card is then submitted to a parent who inspects the finished task and signs the card if he approves the quality of the work. If he does not sign it, the child does the job over on his own time. Cards are turned in at the end of the month and the children are paid the going rate. With the money he earns, each buys his own clothes, except for the youngest, who puts half his money in the bank against the day when he too must take the responsibility for buying clothes.

"We're all working for each other this way," Joe said, "each taking responsibility as he's able. They're not paid, of course, for daily jobs like bedmaking and tablesetting and dishwashing. But last month we paid for 125 hours of 'special' jobs."

Stravinsky in his *Poetics of Music* refers to "the anguish into which an unrestricted freedom plunges me." Unrestricted freedom—anguish. Their opposites, discipline and serenity, characterized the home I've described. But it took thought. It took vision. It took courage to lay the burden on the children, strength to support them in it, humility to submit to the rule of life, and an ear tuned to a different drummer from the one the world hears.

Three Houses, Three Tabernacles

Does the Lord of heaven live in the houses of earth? The prophecies of Isaiah ("Behold, a virgin shall . . . call his name Immanuel") and the Book of Revelation ("Now at last God has his dwelling among man! He will dwell among them and they shall be his people, and God himself will be with them," Rev. 21:3 NEB) are fulfilled every day in the homes of those who love God. I've had some glimpses of this lately, and have been blessed by seeing the presence of God in the homes I've visited.

Scene 1: An apartment in Boston. The young wife is pregnant. Her husband, a stock analyst, has made up his mind to get a dog. Not a manageable, apartment-sized dog, but a nice bouncy big golden retriever that he can run and roughhouse with on the Common. "Oh dear," she says to me, "what am I going to do? I'm having this baby, and the apartment is very small."

We had talked on other occasions about the biblical principle of a wife's submission to her husband. There are times, we agreed, when without disobedience to that command, a wife may offer an alternative viewpoint for her husband's consideration. "I don't want to be a shrew," the young woman said. "The dog and the baby in the apartment with me—can I cope?" I wondered if she could. I felt very sympathetic to her.

So we prayed about it, asking God to give his answer. That very afternoon she called me. "Instant solution! Mike has decided not to get the dog until we can move to a house in the country. And I hadn't even said a word, hadn't suggested that I wasn't sure we could manage! Just wanted you to praise the Lord with me, and Mike doesn't need to know."

Scene 2: Early morning. A polished tile veranda on a hillside overlooking a turquoise sea. There is a cool breeze; birds twitter, chirp and dart among the flowers. Heavy perfume rises from the garden. Two black men are talking quietly nearby, speaking the island patois which I cannot understand. From the open door leading into the cool dark dining room comes a man. He is a big man with big shoulders, broad chest, black hair, and a scarred and deeply lined face. He is wearing jeans and a white shirt this morning, not the black in which the public is accustomed to seeing him. He is Johnny Cash. We talk of the beauty of the morning, of what he's been reading in the Bible, and of June, his wife. I speak of how lovely she is (I met her only yesterday). "She's pure," John says. "That woman has a pure heart." John Carter Cash runs out of the house. He is seven years old, the apple of his father's eye, and the three of us go for a ride in a golf cart before breakfast.

Breakfast is served at a glass table on the east ve-randa by an elegant black man in a white coat. There are six kinds of fruit, including naseberries, an unimpressive brown-skinned sphere with a pulp delectable enough for the gods. The other guests are Billy and Ruth Graham. After breakfast we all go to the beach—John and June, Billy and Ruth, John Carter and Mrs. Kelley who takes care of him, and I. People's faces everywhere light up at once with astonishment and joy—isn't that Johnny Cash? Wow! And—wow again—*that's* Billy Graham! All of them will carry for the rest of their lives a little of the glow.

Finally two teenagers disengage themselves from a knot of friends. "Mr. Graham, could we have your auto-graph?" "Sure. Are those your friends over there? Tell them all to come over." They are ecstatic. I take a color photo (and wonder a week later why it didn't occur to me to take the address of one of the kids. How thrilled they would have been to have a picture of themselves with a famous man!). He is gracious and kind to them. When they go I ask if he is ever irritated by autograph hunt-ers. He laughs. "It isn't a very big thing to do for people, is it?" John says that before he turned his life over to Jesus he was sometimes rude. He got sick of publicity and swarms of hangers-on. "But I'm not living for Johnny Cash now. It has to be different."

Evening. We've had dinner and are sitting in the living room. Gleaming dark wood floors and woodwork. White sofa and chairs, with Wedgewood blue cording. Pale blue draperies, white walls, Oriental rugs, grand piano. John Carter sleeps, sprawled on the sofa beside me in the blissful relaxation of childhood. Eight Jamaicans are there with us—cooks, maids, security men. It is the birthday of Miss Vicki, a cook. June has given her a little collection of presents, and Miss Vicki is asked to lead us in prayer. She does so. Without fuss, without hesitation or self-consciousness, she prays for all of us, calling the Cashes and Grahams her best friends, speaking to God of her responsibility to welcome them and help them, speaking then of the Holy Spirit, asking him to bless us, bless her church, bless our communion together.

" 'Nothing in my hand I bring,' " she quotes, " 'simply to thy cross I cling.' " Then, "I'm like a leaf that the wind blows through. Blow, Holy Spirit."

John strums his guitar, talks a little bit about some of the experiences of his life, and goes into a song, "Why me, Lord?"—a favorite of the prisoners, he says, and they always cry when he sings it. Then he sings "One Day at a Time," and "What on earth will you do for heaven's sake?" The servants sing, too. One by one, opening an old hymnal, they stand and sing, "Peace, peace," "Into my 'eart" (islanders seem to drop h's), "Amazing Grace." Johnny, the "Man in Black," once a drug addict, many times a prisoner, a hard and self-destructive man, listens. He knows well what those simple familiar words mean: "Amazing grace, how sweet the sound that saved a wretch like me." It includes all of us.

Billy reads the Bible—a harmony of the Gospels, giving the Maundy Thursday story since that is what day it is. We pray together. Then June, her great deep eyes earnest, her voice gentle, talks. "Christ dwells in this house," she says, "I know he does. And these people know it." She gestures toward the staff. "When you're here, Elisabeth, you are *covered*. We're all covered— Billy and Ruth, John Carter, Kelley, John, you and I. We're covered by prayer. These people pray for us, don't you?" The Jamaicans nod. "Yes, mum."

John sings some more at our request. "A Boy Named Sue," "Welfare Cadillac," "I Walk the Line." At 9:30 Billy gets up from his chair. "I don't know about y'all, but for me it's bedtime." Everybody gets up.

Ruth and I pause with June and look down at John Carter on the sofa. "I want to tell you about this little boy," June says. "One time John and I were lying in bed just praising the Lord, thanking the Lord, lifting our hands in praise. John Carter was lying there with us, and he lifted up his little hands and said, 'Mama, I think I'm gonna cry!' We all wanted to cry, we were so happy."

During the night a shutter bangs, a dog howls, rain thunders on the roof, and my sunburn wakes me each time I turn over, but I don't mind. It gives me a chance to luxuriate in the huge antique four-poster, to ponder the unthinkable fact that I am in the Cashes' house in Jamaica, a house built in 1740 by the Barretts of Wimpole Street, now the home of a man utterly trans- formed by the grace of God, and a woman whose pray- ers followed him in some of the dark years. ("I wore out the floor praying for him!" June said.)

Next morning we sit by the pool. "I had this passion, this consuming *passion*, to do something with my life, something besides being a wife and mother," June tells us. "I wanted to be a star. I ruined two marriages because of it and I know it. Well—I gave it all up. I gave it up to the Lord, this selfish ambition, and now I have a husband who adores me." (It is obvious that he does.) "So I tell my daughters (and we've got six of them), 'You do like the Bible says. You *submit.* You submit to your husband. If he tells you to get down and scrub floors, buddy, *you hit it!* On all fours if necessary!' "

Scene 3: A doctors' house in San Francisco. In the bedroom are three cribs with three little boys, giggling, cooing, smiling toothlessly, jumping up and down with glee as their mother and I come in. All are about a year old, but they are not triplets. They are adopted and their parents are middle-aged, both of them doctors, the mother nearly fifty. I watch the boys being fed. They get nothing out of baby-food jars. Elizabeth Paeth Lasker (always "Bunny" to me) prepares it herself—pureed chicken and spinach, done in a blender, for lunch, apples and cheese for afternoon snack, salad (salad!) for supper. She lines up three high chairs and starts scooping spoonfuls from a single dish with a single spoon. It is one, two, three, one, two, three. If Number Two spits it out, Number Three gets it. Everybody loves it, everybody is relaxed and exuberant. "Aren't they gorgeous?" Bunny keeps saying. I have never been in a happier home.

Her letter to me last week says, "The children have all had their first birthday now, and so endeth the most eventful and beautiful year of our lives. What a privilege to be this close to these little living, growing persons! There is a constant sacrament of praise as I go through the repeated acts involved in caring for three active little boys. Evelyn Underhill's idea that every temporal act that fills the moments of our day are not just a 'sort' of sacrament but are in fact the *real* sacrament. And since so much of my day is spent in doing little repetitive activities that seem so mean and small, it is somehow cheering and reassuring to think of each of these (scraping messes off rugs, rerolling entire scrolls of toilet paper, changing diapers, washing clothes, making bread, scrubbing sticky floors, scouring high chairs, *ad infinitum*) as a sacrament of praise and *of worth* (incredible!) to the Master."

"The tabernacle of God is with men," and, in the words of John Keble,

The trivial round, the common task,
Will furnish all we ought to ask;
Room to deny ourselves, a road
To bring us daily nearer God.

Notes from a Grandmother's Diary

April 30. I speak today at a theology conference on "Masculinity and Femininity Under God," attempting to show how the question is primarily a theological one for the Christian, not a trivial question of physiology, or merely sociology ("lifestyle," "changing roles," etc.), politics or pragmatics. It must, like all other created matter, *mean* something. I wonder who had "ears to hear"? I fly after the conference from Philadelphia to New Orleans where Walt and my daughter Val meet me, he looking handsome but harried, she radiant, great with child.

May 1. The little cottage in the cane fields is a truly happy home, though the work God has given Walt in the two small churches is well designed to put iron into his soul. Not everybody loves everybody else yet!

Today is their first anniversary. I sit on the sofa and watch Val go through her Lamaze exercises for childbirth, coached and assisted by Walt who attended the classes with her. They are breathing exercises, consisting mainly of alternate panting and puffing in certain prescribed rhythms, an excellent means of distracting a woman's attention from her pain. The concepts of masculinity and femininity find lovely expression here—the man cherishing, protecting, helping, caring for the woman who carries his child; the woman responding to him with all her heart, her body heavy with promise, preparing herself to suffer pain. They have all things in readiness: a room, emptied, painted and furnished, a crib ready to receive; tiny clothes in ordered piles, a white eyelet bag to take to the hospital, containing a diaper or two, a diminutive blue shirt (for a boy) and a rosebud-sprigged gown (it might be a girl, though I think not).

May 4. Today is "due date." Hopes high. A few minor aches that might become pains subside, along with our hopes. If only it could be today, Val would be able to be back home from the hospital on Mother's Day and show off her baby to the eager people at church, some of whom seem much more excited than she. And of course the sooner the baby arrives, the longer his grandmother will be able to help before she has to go off to Minnesota.

May 5. Trying to put together a speech for Minnesota is a difficult business when we are all in suspense. "If we could just get this baby we could get down to business and prepare sermons and things," Walt says.

May 7. Trip to the doctor in New Orleans—a five-hour round trip—for Val's regular weekly check up. Everything fine. No progress. That was his dismaying report.

May 9. The Lord of creation knows all about why it seems to us important that the baby come now. Would it throw off the universe if he were to allow this one child to be born today? Is it too much to ask? What does he know that makes it essential that we wait? Such are the questions I was trying to squelch as I walked in the cane field this afternoon, praying. Sovereign Lord, we await *thy* time. "My times are in thy hand." Thy will be done, in earth, in this corner of the earth, in this young woman, as it is in heaven.

May 12. Every morning I wake with the mockingbirds (and it's a breath-taking concert they perform, beginning at five o'clock in the live oak by my window, chirping, tweeting, whistling, trilling, chipping, warbling, trying out tunes, pulling out different stops) and wonder, *Will it be today?* This is a question Christians ought to be asking every morning about a very different but much longer-awaited event. "Come, Lord Jesus." I go downstairs and start fixing breakfast. Val appears, fresh as a spring stream, no pains, no signs, no complaints. She is eager for the baby but calm in her trust.

. . . It is noon, and still the mockingbird sings, praising God and it seems, mocking me. I sit at a desk near the air conditioner, writing a speech on "The Requirements of Privilege" which I am to deliver to graduating seniors, knowing well that the greatest thing that can be required of anyone is *trust* in the living God. I am not meeting that requirement very satisfactorily if I sit and stew over the way he times things.

May 14. At the doctor's office in New Orleans. It is 10:25 A.M., exactly twenty-four hours since we arrived here for Val's appointment, at which "no progress" was again his report. We drive home, arriving at 10:00 P.M. At 1:15 A.M. Val wakes me. "I'm having them, Mama. Pains every five minutes. I guess we'd better go." Val and Walt are both serene and happy as we drive east. We have clean diapers, a sheet and a pair of freshly boiled scissors in the back of the pickup, just in case. The CB radio is working. As we drive past the cranes, tool shops, tugboats, derricks and welding shops of Morgan City, many pickup trucks are parked outside the bars—a world of men who operate on a different set of hours. *Diesel Hammers, Offshore Welders, Ocean Systems Diving Service* read the signs along the main drag.

Val times her pains with a watch, writes down the intervals and the duration. Three minutes, five minutes, eleven minutes, seven minutes.

"Honey, you're amazing," Walt says. "I love you."

We reach the Huey P. Long Bridge going into New Orleans. The moon shines, a thin sliver with a bright star balanced on its point.

"You all right, honey?" Walt says.

"I'm fine!" Val smiles. She puts her feet in my lap, her head in Walt's. "Praise the Lord, it's happening!" she says.

"You're terrific!"

"But I'm so *happy!*"

We reach Walt's parents' house. Walt tries the door, finds the chain fastened, but almost at once a light goes on in the bedroom. His mother lets us in. I go to bed, Val and Walt decide to go for a walk. At eight I awaken, find everyone asleep. Oh dear, I think, a false alarm. But soon they waken and I am assured that things are still moving. At ten Val calls the doctor. "Come on over," he says. So here we are. . . .

She comes out of the office, smiling a little wistfully.

"He said to go on home. It could be today, maybe tomorrow, maybe Monday."

The afternoon wears away. Val naps, walks, counts

pains, takes a shower. In the evening we go to the hospital.

May 15. 12:40 A.M. I sit in "The Stork Club," the waiting room for expectant fathers. No one else is here. I have just spent forty minutes "spelling" Walt in the labor room, massaging, counting seconds to help Val with her breathing routines, listening to the thrilling amplification of the baby's heartbeat on the monitor. "I understand why they told us this would be the hardest work we'd ever do," Val said.

2:00 A.M. I watch as Walt holds her during one of the hard ones, her head thrown back, anguish on her face, she gasping and puffing according to his quiet instructions. "Honey, you're great!" he says. "You're going to make it!"

3:35 A.M. The doctor arrives at the hospital. Walt goes to don the green garb for the delivery room. Now he comes to the waiting room.

"That daughter of yours!" (I see tears on his cheeks) "She's something! Twenty-seven hours, but she's hanging in there." The nurse calls him.

4:15 A.M. Walt comes to the door (I am no longer alone in the waiting room—a young man and his parents-in-law are there) and beckons me to the hall. He hugs me. "It's a boy. Walter Dorman Shepard III. Hear him? Listen! You can hear him cry down the hall. That's him! That's our son!"

A nurse comes down the hall wheeling a cart. There he is, a tiny, determined face with a dimple in the chin (his mother and father have that dimple, and his grandfather Jim Elliot had it too). We follow the nurse to the nursery where she pushes back the curtains so we can watch her weigh and measure him. We go to Val's room and in a few minutes the nurse brings in the living bundle. The room is quiet.

Mother and child.

The father, bending over them both.

Then he reads the beautiful service for the "Churching of Women" from the Prayer Book:

"O Almighty God, we give thee humble thanks for that thou hast been graciously pleased to preserve, through the great pain and peril of childbirth, this woman, thy servant, who desireth now to offer her praises and thanksgivings unto thee. . . .

"Grant, we beseech thee, O heavenly Father, that the child of this thy servant may daily increase in wisdom and stature, and grow in thy love and service, until he come to thy eternal joy; through Jesus Christ our Lord." We all join in the *Amen*.

The grandmother is thinking also of the lovely words written by Amy Carmichael of India for the children she rescued:

> *Through life's troubled waters steer them,*
> *Through life's bitter battle cheer them.*
> *Father, Father, be thou near them.*

And the grandmother also makes up her mind to try not to talk about this little boy to people who don't ask, and to talk moderately to those who do. But alas, here she is putting it all into words. All? No, she left out quite a lot. And nobody had to read all the way to the end if he didn't want to.

Notes on Prayer

People who ski, I suppose, are people who happen to like skiing, who have time for skiing, who can afford to ski, and who are good at skiing. Recently I found that I often treat prayer as though it were a sport like skiing—something you do if you like it, something you do in your spare time, something you do if you can afford the trouble, something you do if you're good at it. Otherwise you do without it most of the time. When you get in a pinch you try it and then you call an expert.

But prayer isn't a sport. It's work. As soon as I've said that I'm in trouble because so many sports have become professional and as such are almost wholly indistinguishable from work. I could say that work is something you have to decide to do, you have to allow time for, you have to go at with energy, skill and concentration. But all those things could be said of the big business which is sports. Competition is deadly, equipment highly technical and expensive, salaries absurdly high.

But prayer is no game. Even if you are part of a

"team," as when others join you in prayer, you are not cheered on by spectators or coached by any experts. You won't get any trophies—not on this side of the Jordan, anyway. It's not likely you'll get any credit at all. For some people prayer might fall into the category of "fun," but that's not usually the reason we pray. It's a matter of need and responsibility.

Prayer is work because a Christian simply can't "make a living" without it. He can't live a Christian life at all if he doesn't pray.

Prayer is the opposite of leisure. It's something to be engaged in, not indulged in. It's a job you give first priority to, performing not when you have energy left for nothing else. "Pray when you feel like praying," somebody has said. "Pray when you don't feel like praying. Pray until you do feel like praying." If we pray only "at our leisure"—that is, at our own convenience—can we be true disciples? Jesus said, "Anyone who wants to follow me must put aside his own desires and conveniences" (Luke 9:23 LB).

The apostle Paul did use an analogy from sports to describe prayer. He said we "wrestle." In the wrestling of a Christian in prayer, "our fight is not against any physical enemy: it is against organizations and powers that are spiritual. We are up against the unseen power that controls this dark world, and spiritual agents from the very headquarters of evil" (Eph. 6:12, Phillips). Seldom do we consider the nature of our opponent, and that is to his advantage. When we do recognize him for what he is, however, we have an inkling as to why prayer is never easy. It's the weapon that Unseen Power dreads most, and if he can get us to treat it as casually as we treat a pair of skis or a tennis racquet he can keep his hold.

If we're going to ask, *"Is* prayer work?" somebody will want to ask, *"Does* prayer work?" That question assumes that results ought to be measurable. The trouble is they are not by any means always measurable or predictable because the One to whom we address our prayers is infinite and incomprehensible, "and all that is comprehensible about him" (wrote John of Damascus) "is his infinity and incomprehensibility." His thoughts are as much higher than our thoughts as the heavens are higher than the earth.

And he is Love. Infinite Love will never give a stone when bread is asked for, or a scorpion in place of an egg. But what will Infinite Love give if our prayer is for a scorpion?

Prayer is compared in the Bible to incense. "Let my prayer be counted as incense before thee," wrote the Psalmist, and the angel who stood before the altar with the golden censer in Revelation 8 was given incense to mingle with the prayers of the saints. Incense was very expensive, blended by a perfumer according to a strict formula. It appears to serve no particularly useful purpose. Its smoke and fragrance soon dissipate. Couldn't incense be done without?

Prayer is like incense. It costs a great deal. It doesn't seem to accomplish much (as we mortals assess things). It soon dissipates. But God likes the smell. It was God's idea to arrange the work of the tabernacle to include a special altar for incense. We can be pretty sure he included all that was necessary and nothing that was unnecessary.

Christ prayed. He offered thanksgiving, he interceded for others, he made petitions. That the Son—co-equal, co-eternal, consubstantial with the Father—should come to the Father in prayer is a mystery. That we, God's children, should be not only permitted but commanded also to come is a mystery. How can we change things by prayer? How "move" a sovereign and omnipotent God? We do not understand. We simply obey because it is a law of the universe, as we obey other laws of the universe, knowing only that this is how things have been arranged: the book falls to the floor in obedience to the law of gravity if I let go of it. Spiritual power is released through prayer.

I could say, "God can make my hands clean if he wants to," or I could wash them myself. Chances are God *won't* make my hands clean. That's a job he leaves up to me. His omnipotence is not impaired by his having ordained my participation, whether it be in the washing of hands with soap or the helping of a friend with prayer. Christ redeemed the world by the laying down of his life, a perfect sacrifice, once for all. Yet he is in the business, as David Redding says, of "maintenance and repair." He lets us participate with him in that business by the laying down of our own lives.

One way of laying down our lives is by praying for somebody. In prayer I am saying, in effect, "my life for yours." My time, my energy, my thought, my concern, my concentration, my faith—here they are, for you. So it is that I participate in the work of Christ. So it is that no work of faith, no labor of love, no smallest prayer is ever lost, but, like the smoke of the incense on the golden altar, rises from the hand of the angel before God.

Provision for
Sacrifice

I t took me quite a long time to unwrap my breakfast
one day last week. I was flying somewhere—I can't
remember where because the past two months are a
jumble in my memory—checking into TWA, American,
Eastern, Delta; plunking my purse and attaché case
down on the carpeted counter to be sent through the
security scanner; reading the *New Yorker* in boarding
lounges—Atlanta, Cincinnati, San Francisco, Florence,
Grand Rapids; buckling seatbelts; drinking tea and ice
water and (on Allegheny Airlines) apple juice.

Which brings me back to that breakfast flight, wherever it went. I had to unwrap my breakfast. The cutlery
and napkin were sealed in an impregnable plastic bag.
The omelet was encased in gold foil, the muffin in a
paper cup which clung stubbornly. The butter was protected by a square mold of something nearly as tough as
Plexiglass, the orange juice was sealed with a convex
foil lid which when pierced squirted a jet of juice in a
wholly unpredictable direction, and the fruit cup was

fastbound in Saranwrap, the edges, corners and ends of which had been concealed with a cleverness that bordered on the diabolical.

At length, however, the food lay open and exposed to my hunger, and I ate it thankfully. I was thankful, for one thing, to have conquered the wrappings, but genuinely thankful, too, for the luxuries of modern American life—the speed of travel, the comfort of the seat (an economy-class airplane seat is infinitely more comfortable than the two boards at right angles which make up a "first-class" seat on an Ecuadorian banana truck, and I've done my stint on those), the temperature of the cabin when outside it is perhaps seventy degrees below zero, the cleanliness, the quiet, the safety.

All these things, some cynic might point out, are relative. The Concorde travels much faster than a DC-10, a seat in first class is a lot roomier than one in economy class, it is sometimes frigid or stifling on planes, occasionally you find crumbs on your tray table and there is the chance of being seated next to some executive who has just had one of those three-martini lunches or some garrulous grandmother who wants to show you the latest Polaroids of the small person she has just visited. And planes crash, don't forget. So says the cynic.

But it is always possible to be thankful for what is given rather than to complain about what is not given. One or the other becomes a habit of life. There are, of course, complaints which are legitimate—as, for example, when services have been paid for which have not been rendered—but the gifts of God are in an altogether different category. Ingratitude to him amounts (let us resort to no euphemisms) to rebellion.

Many women have told me that my husband's advice, which I once quoted in a book, has been an eye-opener to them. He said that a wife, if she is very generous, may allow that her husband lives up to perhaps eighty percent of her expectations. There is always the other twenty percent that she would like to change, and she may chip away at it for the whole of their married life without reducing it by very much. She may, on the other hand, simply decide to enjoy the eighty percent, and both of them will be happy. It's a down-to-earth illustration of a principle: *Accept, positively and actively, what is given.* Let thanksgiving be the habit of your life.

Such acceptance is not possible without a deep and abiding belief in the sovereign love of God. Either he is in charge, or he is not. Either he loves us, or he does not. If he is in charge and loves us, then whatever is given is subject to his control and is meant ultimately for our joy.

I rode horseback this morning through the sweet fragrance of late autumn woods and meadows, fresh with dew. The New England countryside was a softly muted tapestry of fading color. A few apples still clung to the boughs of gnarled trees. The oak leaves, not yet fallen, were golden banners, and the leaves on the blueberry bushes were still blood red. The horses walked, the saddles creaked, a couple of joyful dogs joined us out of nowhere and capered around the horses as we moved through the meadow. *Thank you, thank you, thank you* was the rhythm of all the world. It was all loveliness, all subject to the will of God, all made for joy.

But I had to come back to my typewriter and remember that there are those for whom today is a burden and a horror. I had intended to write about suffering be-

cause on Sunday I was talking to a group of graduate
students as we sat in my living room after dinner. "How
can we prepare ourselves to suffer?" they had asked,
and as I talked one of them said, "Will you write this
down for us? Will you do an article on it?" And I
thought, yes, perhaps I will do an article. I had been
thinking very much about suffering in the past two
weeks because it seemed I had encountered more of it in
more of its varied forms, in the lives of people I had met,
than in any other short period of my life. A couple whose
only son had died of bone cancer. A woman who said to
me with tears on her cheeks, "I am losing my husband—
but in another way from the way you lost yours. But it's
all right." A woman with a grotesquely disfiguring
disease which had plagued her for more than twenty
years. A couple whose two-year-old son choked to death
on an almond. A woman whose oldest son died in a
motorcycle accident six weeks ago—"and am I angry at
God? *Oh God*, am I angry!" she said. A widow left with
millions of dollars in debts. And tonight, only a few
hours after that beautiful ride through the woods, I
listened to a father tell of appalling things his children
have done and are doing which break his heart. His voice
broke, his hands tried to find something to do to hide
their trembling as he talked.

In the days of Cyrus, when the temple was restored in
Jerusalem, he decreed that all that was needed for sacrifice, the young bulls, rams or sheep for burnt offerings
to the God of heaven, wheat, salt, wine or oil, should be
given "day by day without fail." Is it not reasonable to
believe that that same God, the God of heaven to whom

all thanks is due, will provide for us today the materials for sacrifice? "All things come of thee, O Lord," we sing, "and of thine own have we given thee."

Sometimes the materials he provides are things of beauty, things for which we give thanks at once with all our being. The glory of the oak trees today was one of these. And sometimes they are things which break our hearts—not gifts in the sense that Almighty God decrees the evil and suffering of the world (we only know *that* he allowed it, we do not know *why*), but gifts in that he gives to us himself—his presence, his never-failing love in the midst of our pain. We may offer up those very pains, those inexplicable catastrophes that baffle us to silence. We may even give him our broken hearts, for the sacrifices of God, we are told, are "a broken spirit, a broken and a contrite heart." All of it—the gladness and the sorrow—material for sacrifice, given "day by day without fail." For one who has made thanksgiving the habit of his life, the morning prayer will be, "Lord, what will you give me today to offer back to you?"

A Convention,
a Winter Storm
and a Wedding

It is a dark winter morning. The hemlocks outside my window sag with snow, and the driveway is covered. I have just called Mr. Tognazzi to make sure he still has my name on his list for plowing. I shoveled three times yesterday, but only succeeded in clearing the flagstone walk and the steps, and this morning it was hard to tell I had done anything at all.

But I love being shut in with snow. There is a quietness and a more deliberate pace to life. The cars move more quietly and more slowly on the road beyond the hemlocks. MacDuff, my Scottish terrier, limits himself to a few trails he has made in the backyard, and often just sits motionless in a saucer of snow, letting the falling flakes frost his ragged black coat and beard.

This winter morning is a space of peace between two very attention absorbing events. One took place several weeks ago in Houston. On one side of town the International Women's Year Convention was being held. People like Bella Abzug, Betty Friedan, Gloria Steinem and

Margaret Mead were there, along with thousands (reports ranged from eight to eighteen thousand) of others, some of them delegates elected in the state IWY conventions held earlier. Betty Ford, Rosalynn Carter and Lady Bird Johnson were there, too—but *can* they have fully apprehended what the convention was about? *Did* they read the small print of the amendment? The IWY was asking for the passage of the Equal Rights Amendment, for lesbian rights (which would include the right of homosexual couples to marry and/or to adopt children), for federally funded abortion and other related issues.

Across town fifteen thousand people packed the AstroArena, built to accommodate far fewer, and several thousand were turned away. They were there for a Pro-Family Rally, an orderly attempt to register in the mind of the public an awareness that the IWY was not a true representation of American women. Bella's crowd had a right to speak their piece, but they had no right to speak for all of us. I was one of many speakers at the Pro-Family Rally, and I had been given eight minutes in which to present a Christian view of womanhood. Phyllis Schlafly of Eagle Forum, dedicated to stopping the ERA, spoke, thanking those who had organized the convention, and then thanking her husband Fred for *letting* her come (italics hers). She went on to explain why the ERA was neither necessary nor desirable, e.g., all the legislation needed to give women equal employment opportunity and equal pay has already been passed; ERA will infringe on the rights of women to be protected from military service and supported as wives and mothers.

Representative Clay Smothers called for "segregation"—from perverts and misfits—in our educational system; Dr. Mildred Jefferson, the first black woman to graduate from Harvard Medical School, spoke eloquently against abortion. Banners bore such slogans as *Lesbians—you don't represent women! ERA is a turkey! Family rights are women's rights*, and a father carried a baby who was holding up a sign, *I was a fetus once*. A band played, a group of girls dressed in red, white and blue and carrying big black Bibles sang, a soloist wearing a dazzling yellow suit with a red shirt sang, "When you pray, pray for a miracle," and another soloist led the entire mob in singing "God Bless America."

It was my first convention that resembled a political one, and to see the Bible being waved and to hear the shouts of *Praise the Lord!* that punctuated the speeches surprised me. It even moved me nearly to tears. Where is our country going when the notion of "equal rights" can mean the introduction of homosexual literature into public schools "to give children options in sexual preference"? Somebody from IWY called it a "low blow" when the Pro-Family group ran an advertisement headed, "Mommie, when I grow up can I be a lesbian?", yet it is a true and sobering illustration of what could happen in the kind of world the IWY seeks to create, a murky wasteland, a hideous anarchy where God-given distinctions are obfuscated or even reversed.

When I returned to my hotel room that evening I watched some of the television coverage. There were hours of IWY, with now and then a minute or two of Pro-Family. Viewers could only conclude that the Pro-

Family rally was a fringe group of dissidents, far out-numbered by the allegedly representative group at the IWY. What view President Carter and the lawmakers of the nation will take of what happened in Houston re-mains to be seen. Many thousands of American women pray for the defeat of the Equal Rights Amendment and the preservation by law of sexual distinction so essential to freedom of religion, freedom to build Christian homes, and freedom to be whole men and whole women under God.

The snow has turned to freezing rain now, and the trees bend with the weight of the ice which forms on their branches. Every twig is glazed; every frond of evergreen is cut crystal. I hope my pink dogwood and my two poor little peach trees, so wounded by last year's storms, will not be done in by this one. A small hope and a trivial fear by comparison with my hopes and fears for this beloved country of ours, but I bring both kinds to him who alone can do something about weather and human nature. Psalm 147 is a song of praise:

> *He showers down snow, white as wool, and sprink-*
> *les hoar-frost thick as ashes;*
> *crystals of ice he scatters like breadcrumbs;*
> *He utters his word, and the ice is melted.*
> *O praise the Lord.*

Ice, hoarfrost, snow. The earth, its realms, its cities. The wounds and broken spirits of his people. All of these subject to his command, affected by the word. He who heals and binds up, who brings peace and sends his command, who scatters crystals of ice like breadcrumbs and then speaks to melt them—he is still in charge.

He is in control of the other event which absorbs my attention with more urgency now than did the Houston convention. It is a wedding. And the wedding is mine. One week from today in a small Gothic chapel with a few friends and family members I will be entering into what the 1662 Prayer Book calls "Holy Matrimony, signifying unto us the mystical union that is betwixt Christ and his Church . . . not by any to be enterprised, nor taken in hand, unadvisedly, lightly, or wantonly, but reverently, discreetly, advisedly, soberly, and in the fear of God."

And, may I add, with unspeakable thanksgiving. For me it is the third time—for me who was sure she was a "one-man woman," for me who thought it a miracle even the first time that any man would want her. But God, whose judgments are unsearchable, gave two and took away two in death, so that his giving a third seems beyond all imagining. I will be making those vows advisedly and soberly, to be sure: "To obey, serve, love, honour, and keep him in sickness and in health; and, forsaking all other, keep me only unto him, so long as we both shall live." Even for the third time, there are thrills; *because* it's the third time, there is also a deeper solemnity.

I know why vows, not pleasant sentiments, are required. G. K. Chesterton said they are "a yoke imposed by all lovers on themselves. It is the nature of love to bind itself, and the institution of marriage merely paid the average man the compliment of taking him at his word. Modern [Chesterton wrote more than seventy years ago] sages offer to the lover, with an ill-flavored grin, the largest liberties and the fullest irresponsibility; but they do not respect him as the old Church respected him; they do not write his oath upon the heavens as the record of his highest moment. They give him every liberty except the liberty to sell his liberty, which is the only one that he wants. . . . It will not work. There are thrilling moments, doubtless, for the spectator, the amateur and the aesthete; but there is one thrill that is known only to the soldier who fights for his own flag, to the ascetic who starves himself for his own illumination, to the lover who makes finally his own choice. And it is this transfiguring self-discipline that makes the vow a truly sane thing."

Love Has a Price Tag

It is early morning. I lie as usual in a double bed, and as usual I wake and give thanks for the sleep and safety of the night, for health and warmth and food and friends, for work to do and strength to do it. There is, as before, a layer of silence above the distant sound of traffic.

There are some other sounds as well, not usual at all—instead of the sharp, peremptory bark of MacDuff I hear the muted and mournful howl of Johnny Reb, a beagle who belongs to the next-door neighbors. The garbage truck grinds up the hill outside my window (for this house is on a hill). And there is the sound of someone breathing—beside me.

Lord, Father of Spirits, Lover of Souls, my Light and my Stronghold, thanks! Thanks for the greatest of earthly blessings, marriage.

My prayer goes on for a little while—thanksgiving and petition (that I may be the sort of wife I ought to be, that together we may accomplish the will of the Father).

Later in the kitchen while I fix breakfast I think about this business of being transplanted. We have a nice little brick house on a very quiet street with a view of the Atlanta skyline from the kitchen windows.

Usually to get married means to be transplanted. Always it means to hand over power. Our Lord has a sense of humor, and he has heard me over the past couple of years as I went around talking about marriage, "popping off" about how a woman is supposed to behave toward a man. He has "read" my book, too, I'm sure— *Let Me Be a Woman*. He knows, too, that I believed every word of it, believed it was the truth of God that I spoke.

"All right," he said, "try it again."

He gave me a third husband four-and-a-half years after the death of the second, and he said, "Did you really believe all those things you said and wrote? Have another go at it to make sure."

Love means self-giving. Self-giving means sacrifice. Sacrifice means death. Those are some of the things I've said. I got them out of the same Book, the only thoroughly and eternally reliable Sourcebook. The principles of gain through loss, of joy through sorrow, of getting by giving, of fulfillment by laying down, of life out of death is what that Book teaches, and the people who have believed it enough to live it out in simple, humble, day-by-day practice are people who have found the gain, the joy, the getting, the fulfillment, the life. I really do believe that.

"Lord," I ask, "help me to live it out."

"All right," he says to me, "here's your chance."

In Georgia.

Georgia, where I'm the one with the accent. They call me "Lizbeth." They "carry" children to school or friends to the airport, they don't "take" them. Photographers "make" rather than "take" pictures. They drink "Co-Cola," they go to "fillin' stations," they eat "congealed" salads, and words like *spin* and *hill* have two long-drawn-out syllables.

Sometimes we can trace strange connections in the patterns God works in human lives. One of the last things Add Leitch said to me was that if God should restore him to health he would like to become a hospital chaplain. My new husband is a hospital chaplain.

He took me to Milledgeville to visit the women in the geriatric ward.

"How ya doin', Miz Jackson?"

"Tol'ble well, tol'ble well, preacher. Come here, Ah'm'on' pray for you."

She rises, slowly and painfully, from her chair, places her hands on his shoulders, and repeats with deep fervor the whole of the Lord's prayer.

A woman with beautiful white hair sits in a wheelchair that is hung with more than a dozen pouches, purses and drawstring bags. She quotes from Chaucer's *Canterbury Tales*, talks knowledgeably of Canterbury Cathedral, of Henry VIII, and Cranmer's Prayer Book, winking at me as she talks, as though the two of us are privy to something Lars doesn't know.

We eat breakfast with Mr. Smith, a very handsome man with white hair, ruddy skin and bright blue eyes. He is wearing a blue shirt and blue sweater. He tells us a story which brings into sharp focus the words of the wedding vows—"in sickness and in health, for better, for worse." His wife has been a patient at Milledgeville for three years.

"When she first got sick I carried her everywhere. I did. The doctor said, 'She'll get worse, every week and every month. So if you want to go on any trips or anywhere, go now.' We had some good times, me and her. But the doctor said, 'You cain't stand it. You won't be able to stand it.' Well, I said, 'Ah'm'on' hang on long's I can.'

"I took care of her for five years, but I lost fifty-two pounds just from worry. I was so tense they broke three needles tryin' to put a shot in my arm. Well, I carried her to twenty-five doctors but they couldn't do nothin'. It's brain deter'ation, they told me. I did everything for her. I dressed her and fed her and everything, but it like to whup me and if it hadn't of been for the good Lord I'da never made it. Doctor said, 'I'da sworn you'd never last six months.' But a lot of people were prayin' for me. Oh yes. But finally I had to give up and put her here.

"She cain't do nothin.' Cain't move or speak or hear. She's in the prebirth position, legs and arms locked, heels locked up tight behind. You cain't *straighten* her out. But I come every other day. I go in and kiss her 'bout a dozen times, jes' love her to death. I talk to her. She don't hear, but she knows my touch.

"Well." Mr. Smith finished his story. "I work for the florist here. Volunteer work, you know. I go around the wards, carrying flowers."

We went later to see Mrs. Smith. If ever there was a

sight to confound a man's love for a woman, to strain to the breaking point the most potent human passion, we saw it in that stark white crib—a crumpled scrap of inert humanity. But there is a love that is strong as death, a love many waters cannot quench, floods cannot drown.

I thought of that kind of love not long afterwards, and I thought of it with shame, for I had been disturbed by a petty thing. It is sweet Georgia springtime now, lavish compensation for January's cold, and the birds sing. But I, being still a sinner, can be disturbed by a petty thing. Back I went to the Sourcebook, to the thirteenth chapter of 1 Corinthians, for a clear description of how I ought to act if I really wanted my prayer answered ("Make me the sort of wife I ought to be").

What I found was the precise opposite of my own inclinations in this instance, because this time I was quite sure that my husband was wrong. Reading my own name in place of the word *love*, followed by the opposites of each characteristic described, I saw my own face in the glass and the truth knocked me down. "E. loses patience, is destructive, possessive, anxious to impress, cherishes inflated ideas of her own importance, has bad manners, pursues selfish advantage, is touchy, keeps account of evil. . . ."

I couldn't go on. The antidote to these horrors was love—the kind that "knows no limit to its endurance, no end to its trust, no fading of its hope; it can outlast anything. It is, in fact, the one thing that still stands when all else has fallen."

The Word of God is light, and in its light we see light. My perspective changed; I saw what had bothered me as a petty thing, as nothing. Peace and equilibrium were restored—and that without a "sharing" session. "Thy words were found and I did eat them, and they were unto me the *joy* and *rejoicing* of my heart." "Thy statutes have been my *songs* in the house of my pilgrimage." Thanks be to God for such songs.

Never Frustrated

The first time I saw her she had her back to me as she stood washing dishes at the kitchen sink. She was wearing a dress with a small black and white print, and an apron. She had a slight hump between her shoulders, gray hair, and I could see the wire for her hearing aid running down over her left shoulder. I said something to her but she did not respond.

"She's deaf," my sister said in a loud voice. I thought it was rather too loud a voice, and asked (softly), "You mean she can't hear a thing?" *"Not even if you shout!"* Ginny shouted. It was true. Mrs. Kershaw couldn't hear even if you shouted—unless you shouted directly into the tiny microphone she kept pinned to her dress.

I touched her shoulder, and she turned to me and smiled. "Oh, here she is!" she said, in a flat, nasal tone and a slight lisp. She had heard about the daughter who was away at college, and her smile of welcome was pure radiance in the wrinkled sweet face.

Mrs. Kershaw was a widow who had come to help my

mother. She was quite literally a godsend. Over the years Mother had had a succession of "helpers" who were usually more liability than asset. (One of them met her at the front door when she came home after a shopping trip with, "Oh, Mrs. Howard, I have a surprise for you!" Mother's heart sank. The girl had spent the day, instead of at the tasks assigned, painting her room—woodwork and furniture—shiny chocolate brown.)

God must have seen that Mother had learned her lessons of patience and humility and deserved at last one of his saints, a woman utterly without guile, ambition, touchiness or egotism of any sort. Dear Mrs. Kershaw! When we get together for family reunions we always talk about her. We remember how . . .

She lived alone in a big old wooden house a couple of miles from our home. One of us would pick her up in the car every morning and take her home in the evening. Usually she was at the door, ready to come out when the car arrived. Once in a while we went to the door. There would be a sign on it: "I am home. Please come in." She could not, of course, hear a knock or a doorbell or the telephone. If you wanted her, you had to walk in and find her. She was never afraid the wrong person might want her.

When she got into the car she said what a nice day it was. If the sun shone she said, "Folks can do things outside, work in their gardens." When it rained she said, "Gives folks a chance to do what they wants."

We were sitting at the lunch table in the kitchen one day when a painter was climbing around outside the window. "Gets around pretty soup-le!" she remarked, meaning supple.

One evening at dinner (she always sat at the table with us) the discussion was about Bible names. Five out of us six children had Bible names and Mrs. Kershaw thought this was such a nice idea. My father kept her in on the conversation by speaking into the microphone which she held out to him. She smiled and nodded. Next evening, apropos of nothing, she said, "Harrison isn't in the Bible. I looked him up." Bless her heart! Her only child was named Harrison, a middle-aged man by then.

We always had family Bible reading after dinner. One evening my father said he would read from 1 Thessalonians. "That's a nice book," Mrs. Kershaw said. Nobody answered her remark, partly because we were supposed to be quiet for the reading, and partly because nobody could easily reply—we would have had to ask for the microphone. She looked around the table inquiringly; then, supposing that our silence might indicate disagreement, she said, "I don't know whether it's any good or not, but I like it." We smiled and nodded our agreement and she settled back with a contented sigh.

She often took care of a man who was in his nineties, and she would tell us about him. He was inclined to be a bit crotchety and unpredictable, but she said, "When they gets old they gets that way sometimes. Hope I'm not that way when I get old." She was in her mid-seventies but not, in her mind, even approaching "old."

She would spend hours sitting with my step-grandmother who lived with us and was confined to her room upstairs. Nana was quite deaf, too, so the two of them would chatter away, often at cross-purposes, but not minding, Mrs. Kershaw doing her best to cheer up an otherwise very gloomy lady not much older than herself. Once my father overheard a conversation between Mrs. Kershaw and a Belgian lady who was visiting us who did not speak English. The answers did not match the questions at all, but he let them alone until he heard Mrs. Kershaw repeating several times, "What is your name?" The Belgian lady, by guesswork, figured out what she was asking and replied, "Victorine." "Oh," said Mrs. Kershaw, "Freda. That's a nice name." At that my father felt it was time to help out.

Mrs. Kershaw was not a great cook, but she knew how to make applesauce and brown sugar cookies. The gallons of the former and dozens of the latter were consumed as fast as she could turn them out. She could do plain country cooking—meat, potatoes and vegetables—and she loved to see us eat. One of my brothers spurned the cabbage on his plate. She begged him to eat it. "Why don't you like cabbage? You like chicken, don't you?" she said. Often her comments amused us beyond concealment but she always laughed with us, looking eagerly around the circle for any clues, confident, I feel sure, that she knew we were all crazy about her.

She did get old, finally. I suppose she was well along in her eighties when she had to go and live with Harrison in a tiny cramped room, so packed with her furniture and boxes and things that she could hardly move. I visited her there in a little town some distance from ours. "They calls it a clam town," she said of the village near the New Jersey shore. "Well, I call it a clam town, too—the people just kinda clams up, you know. Yes. Not friendly. They're not friendly at all." They don't know what they missed.

If ever a woman accepted the demands of her own life with simplicity and grace, it was she. It was a positive and active acceptance of the *given*. Words which have taken hold of our minds today like some noxious fungus—hassle, frustration, hang-up, put-down—were never in Mrs. Kershaw's vocabulary, nor could they have been. She wasn't interested in herself. She had nothing to say about herself or her own feelings. She lived for us.

I think of the contrasts Paul speaks about in 1 Corinthians 4. It is illuminating to set them in two lists and read straight down one list, then read down the other and ask oneself which describes his own life.

handicapped	never frustrated
puzzled	never in despair
persecuted	never have to stand it alone
knocked down	never knocked out

"We know sorrow, yet our joy is inextinguishable. We have 'nothing to bless ourselves with,' yet we bless many others with true riches. We are penniless, and yet in reality we have everything worth having."

For Paul to have said that—Paul, who had suffered the loss of all things—ought to shake up our categories of what is "worth having." Mrs. Kershaw would have said the same. I doubt that it ever occurred to her that she had been deprived of anything in her life that really mattered. The Lord had made his face to shine upon her and had given her peace, and she brought that shine and that peace to our house every day.

Darkness Never Conquers Light

I spent all day today at the Shore Country Day School Annual Fair and Sale. A huge bash, enormous fun, all the parents pitching in enthusiastically to sell hot dogs and manage games. There were balloons, pompoms and crepe paper all fluttering about, music playing, pie-eating contests, cream-pie-throwing contests (the teachers volunteered their faces as targets), raffles, etc. My job was to oversee the antique car ride. The car in question was a three-quarter size scale model of a 1903 car with a tiny gas engine that putted along at six miles per hour. The tots drove it, with one of the fathers 'riding shotgun' on the running board. . . ."

This is from a letter I received from one of my four brothers not many weeks ago. I hear from all of them, and from my sister and mother as well, quite regularly. Few people, it seems, correspond regularly with anybody nowadays, let alone with their own relatives. Crowded lives, expensive postage and the convenience of long-distance phone calls are the usual excuses.

But we have always kept up with each other, thanks to our mother who when we first went off to boarding school began sending copies of our letters around to the others. As the years passed we began to make it a little easier for her by making carbons of our letters, and week after week, year in and year out, she takes a good-sized chunk of her time to sort and stuff copies into envelopes, which she addresses and stamps and sends off around the world—always including her own cheerful newsy page, on which nearly every sentence is an exclamation! Or a double exclamation!! Or contains words written in CAPITAL LETTERS!!!

There was another paragraph in my brother's letter, very different from the first: "This week I drove to Children's Hospital in Boston to chauffeur a mother and her little boy, who has acute leukemia. The child is having (1) radiation on the brain, (2) chemotherapy and (3) some dreadful spinal injections in the bargain.

"The scene in the playroom where all the little children come with their mothers to wait for their 'medicine' (that seems to be the term) is too much: all these little, bald, gray, elfin *phantoms*, peering out of brown-ringed eyes. One tiny girl with a cane. Little tots with stuffed frogs and teddy bears clutched under their arms. Bone-chilling screams coming from the room labeled 'Special Procedures' (read spinal taps and marrow scrapings, I guess).

"A whole room full of beds where they sit, propped up, while the lethal chemicals drip through plastic tubes into their veins. One teen-age girl lying on her side in that room, quietly, with tears dropping slowly across the bridge of her nose. One colored baby with just enough hair left for her mother to have arranged two pigtails exactly the thickness of twisted black sewing thread about three inches long."

A letter came in that same mail from another brother: "'Twas the eighteenth of April in seventy-five. . . .' Yet two hundred years later I am sitting in a hotel almost in sight of the infamous Berlin wall that represents the opposite of all that Paul Revere stood for. Yesterday I crossed that wall into East Berlin, and from the time I entered with stony guards carefully scrutinizing me and my passport until I came out—again under the cold eyes of sullen-faced guards—I never saw a smile from one official.

"By contrast I spent lunch and all afternoon with a group of six joyful, hearty pastors and Christian leaders who hugged me, gave me strong handshakes, joked, prayed earnestly, spoke words of encouragement *to me* (yes, not vice versa), promised to pray for me, pronounced a benediction on me at our parting.

"One man said, 'Everything is gray here, no color.' That is both literally and symbolically true. Very little color on the streets, buildings still pock-marked with shells from street fighting at the end of World War II. Gray, sad faces. Another said, 'You can only be a happy man in this country if you know Jesus.' 'Here you are either a Christian or not a Christian. No middle ground. When we don't have outward liberty we learn more of true liberty in Jesus.' "

The juxtaposition in a few paragraphs of these scenes—gaiety, anguish, persecution—read through hurriedly one morning as I opened a pile of mail, brought once again the insistent question of God's meaning and purpose. What does he want of us? How, finding himself in such starkly opposing frameworks, is the Christian to respond to God? Is it best, perhaps, to try not to think about him when one is watching a pie-throwing contest? Ought one to try not to think—better still, to try not even to *see* anything at all—when one has to enter a children's cancer ward? Shall we not even read about the suffering on the other side of the Wall? But that is not accepting life. It is evasion. Those Eastern European Christians are not evading, they are rejoicing. How can it be?

Another letter came to me, this one from a young woman I do not know: "This year the Concerts and Lectures Committee at the college I attend has sponsored a series of lectures concerning the topic, 'What Future for My Generation?' Yesterday the guest speaker was the black activist Stokely Charmichael. Although I have been upset about the direction our world seems to be heading, his talk along with the others has prompted me to write to you.

"I am getting married in June. My question is this: What responsibility do you feel a Christain couple has in regard to having children? . . . I know the Lord is totally in charge of the future, but it frightens me to think of my part in bringing a child into an unhappy and unstable world."

Music, balloons, cream pies. Brain tumors, barbed wire, death. This is the world we live in. Ever since the Garden of Eden was sullied by evil it has been an unhappy and an unstable world. Has it ever been right to bring a child into such a world? For the Christian it is right—a thousand times right. For it is the will of God that married people accept the responsibility of children. It is the will of God that we live in the world—this world of light and darkness, of gladness and suffering—for it is this world that Jesus Christ came to redeem. Christianity, alone among the religions of the world, looks steadfastly at the facts, whatever they may be, and says there is an ultimate explanation, an ultimate purpose, a glorious answer.

"Everything belongs to you!" Paul said. "The world, life, death, the present, or the future—everything is yours, for you belong to Christ, and Christ belongs to God."

We cannot protect the child we bring into the world. ("This, this is the victory of the grave; here is death's sting, that it is not strong enough, our strongest wing," wrote the poet Charlotte Mew. "But what of His who like a Father pitieth? His Son was also, once, a little thing. . . .") But we can bring him to the Cross, where all longings, all hopes and failures, all sin and sadness and pain and fear are gathered up in everlasting love and transformed for us forever into glory and beauty and joy.

So what about the country fair? Try to keep God out of it? Why? *He* is watching it. He sees *us* watching it. Does he mind that we have a hilarious time? "Everything belongs to you!" Try thanking him.

And what of the children with the tubes running into them? He sees them. He loves them. He has not finished yet with their redemption. Can we watch with him—watch and pray and hold them up to everlasting love?

And the prisoners and exiles—they, too, are in his plan. "God has no problems," Corrie ten Boom says, "only plans." We suffer with them because they are members of the same Body, but our Christian faith enables us to look steadfastly and not hide our eyes, to pray earnestly and not despair, because Jesus commanded us: "Be of good cheer. *I have overcome the world!*"

Junk Food

If you're hungry, the airport in Fayetteville, Arkansas, is not a good place to be. The selection of "snacks" in the vending machine is impressive, but there is nothing at all that one could call food. You can insert your quarters, nickels and dimes (no pennies) and get chocolate chip cookies, potato chips (plain), potato chips with "bar-B-Q" flavor, potato chips with sour cream and onion (artificial) flavor, potato "Stix," pork rinds, corn chips, "Cornies," "Pub Fries," "Cheddar Fries," "Cheetos," "Cheese Smackers," and things called "Doritos," "Bugles," "Jammers" and "Dunkums."

Alongside that machine is another one offering brightly colored aluminum cans of sweet fizzy stuff with which to wash down all those snacks—or, I suppose, to Dunkum. I don't like to contemplate what state your blood sugar or your nerves or your sanctification would be in if your supper comprised a Tab and a package of Jammers, but on second thought, a look around the boarding lounge of almost any airport—at the facial expressions, the behavior of the pre-school-age tots, and the remarks overheard—give a clue. We are a nation "overfed but undernourished," to borrow the title of Curtis Wood's book.

Junk food is not nourishment. It's easily available (if you have the right coins). It is packaged up in eye-catching wrappings, presumably untouched by human hands. It can be transported to plane, to beach, to movie theatre, to school, to bed. It can be grabbed in a moment, wolfed down on the run; and there are no preparations to make, nothing to clean up except greasy fingers. It does away altogether with the *ritual* of eating—the laid table, the attractive presentation of a dish, the fellowship with others, the leisure to enjoy. In a world that has lost or discarded nearly all other rituals, what will become of us if we do away with even this one?

But worst of all, junk food feeds (feeding will make you fat) but does not nourish. Nourishment makes you strong. I sat on the molded fiberglass seat in Fayetteville, waiting for the small plane which would take me to Tulsa, and wished for a few crunchy fat Bing cherries or a slice of the wheat-honey bread that I make regularly at home—real food.

Don't misunderstand. I like potato chips. I like Cheetos. I haven't tried the commercially packaged pork rinds, but I certainly enjoyed the kind the Indians gave me in South America—fished out of a cauldron of hot fat bubbling over an open fire in some jungle clearing, eaten with a chunk of steamed manioc or a plantain roasted in the ashes.

We are people of our times and culture. Because of

the "schedule" I seem to be obliged to keep, I am always looking for ways to use my time more efficiently, and one of them is to listen to tapes while I do my hair and face. I switched the recorder off the other day, disgusted with what I told my husband was spiritual junk food. A man was rambling on about his own feelings, his "meaningful" experiences, and how he got in touch with himself, with other people, and with God. No doubt he was telling the truth, but there wasn't a single reference to Scripture, and not much there that would nourish me.

Christian bookstores usually carry some real "meat," if you can find it. It is not likely to be up front where the paperbacks, the tapes and the records are, which display on their jackets color photographs of the author, the speaker or the singer, often taken in an open meadow, in a soft, misty light, and with a few wildflowers. (Are there any analogies here—artificial color, perhaps, or flavor? What about preservatives? I understand preservatives are used in foods to give a longer "shelf life." The booksellers have thought of some tricks, I'm sure, to keep their wares in the public eye for a few weeks longer, but no trick takes the place of quality for preserving a book's shelf life.)

Tastes are developed. Solzhenitsyn, in his speech at Harvard a few months ago, deplored the "TV stupor" in which Americans live. He spoke of the decadence of art, of intolerable music, of mass prejudice, spiritual exhaustion, material luxury, and a morally inferior happiness. He is right. Alas, his own experience of totalitarianism and concentration camp gives him the perspective and the authority to judge our society. We must hear him.

Doctors have been learning of the physical exhaustion that can result from artificial or refined or highly sugared foods. Might not one cause of the spiritual exhaustion which Solzhenitsyn observes be the spiritual junk food we consume? What shall be done for the child fed on the snack-pack, the soft drink and the TV dinner? Will he never choose, let alone enjoy, vegetables? Will the Christian whose spiritual sustenance has been limited to the mass-produced, who is accustomed only to "snacking," whose tastes have been conditioned by the majority, ever choose what is truly nourishing?

What it comes down to, with regard to spiritual things, is that we ought to learn to do some of our own cooking. Granted, it is much easier to grab a package. But sometimes we ought to start from scratch.

Let us start with silence. That may be the hardest thing to achieve in our world. But it is not impossible. For one thing, it takes the will to be quiet. It is possible to be quiet on a crowded subway or in the kitchen when the bacon is frying, the washing machine is running and the baby wants more milk. It is easier by far to be quiet when things around us are quiet, and for most of us this means getting up early.

I was in my study this morning before the traffic had started up on Route 1A. No sound came from the road or the house. Only the sweet susurrus of the crickets in the grass and the cawing of a crow in a beech tree broke the silence, yet it took also an act of the will to be still and know that He is God. My mind races quite naturally over things done yesterday (burying a beloved friend's beloved little dog, getting my sister from the hospital, swimming in the ocean, writing a page or two) or things to be done today (writing more than a page or two, having a friend to tea, getting my mother from the airport). Be still. It is a command. The Hebrew word used in Psalm 46 can mean "Shut up."

The great books that have been spiritual meat and drink for me have been produced, I feel sure, out of great silence. Men and women of God have learned of him by being quiet and allowing him to speak to them in their solitude. They have been willing to be alone, to shut up, to listen, and to think and pray over what they have heard. In our modern world most people choose noise. Go to the beach or a forest camp and find portable radios, television sets, record players. Sit down in a waiting room and listen to what Malcolm Muggeridge calls that "drooling mélange" of Muzak. People want noise. They would far rather discuss than think, talk over their problems than pray about them, read a paperback about what somebody else thinks about the Bible than read the Bible.

We cannot stand stillness. Yet we need it. I wonder if the popularity of transcendental meditation is due to this felt need. Whatever may be said about TM's being a religion or not, the measure of success it seems to enjoy could be attributed in part to the simple fact that its devotees spend a certain amount of time daily in motionless silence. That can't hurt anybody.

As one of those who write the stuff that is for sale in the bookstores I referred to, I know that responsibility is laid upon me to provide real food. So I speak to myself— I must do my own "cooking." It is not fast food that I ought to provide for my reader. I must feed him, but in order to do that I must myself be fed. What I speak or write must come out of silence where only a still small voice can be heard.

I speak also to my reader. Seek what is good for the soul, even if it doesn't come in paperback. Read an old book once in a while. (Try P. T. Forsyth, *The Principle of Authority*, or Luther's *Letters of Spiritual Counsel*.) And once in a while lay aside the books and the tapes. For a set period of time be alone, be still. "The man who lives on me will live because of me," Jesus said. *"This* is the bread which came down from heaven."

Little Black Dog

I t is a late October morning of glorious sunshine in New Hampshire and I sit in an antique rocking chair by the window of an old house which was once a barn. The gray rocks on Mount Lafayette's broad summit are dusted with snow, and the sky is as blue as a sky can be. All that is still green today is the evergreens. Between them are the black line drawings of the thin leafless maples, wild cherries, aspens and birches. The feathery tamaracks are dark gold. Little yellow apples hang on one of the gnarled old trees of the orchard. I keep hoping a deer will come for them.

My friend Miriam and I drove up yesterday from Boston for a few days of quiet at my brother's place. Both of us brought a load of desk work. No one else is here except Daisy, Miriam's new friend, a little white Pekingese. (Her old friend, Pity Sing, died a few weeks ago.)

MacDuff, my six-year-old Scottish terrier, is not here this time either. We went for a short climb yesterday afternoon, up a rocky wooded trail that he used to love. He would race after the chattering chipmunks, bound up the steep granite slabs, and wait, panting, at the top for us to catch up. I missed him yesterday on that trail. I miss him today when I look out of the window.

MacDuff died of cancer last week. I knew he was sick during the summer when his routines changed. He sat in the middle of the back yard one morning, instead of in his usual place by the fence, looking bewildered instead of in charge. One rainy day he was not on his chair in the screened porch, but I found him lying in a hollow place under a bush. He no longer leaped for his Milk-Bone at the breakfast table. But he kept his ears and tail up, and thus kept my hopes up.

The vet said he had an infection and gave us pills. MacDuff got very cagey at detecting where those pills had been hidden in his food, so I had to try ever sneakier methods of getting them into him. They worked fine. He was well again—for a while—faithfully putting in his self-appointed barking time each day, letting neighbor dogs know who was in charge, and keeping off trespassers, some of whom must have been demons since none of us humans could see them.

But I saw that he was losing weight. I could feel the shoulder blades and spine through his heavy, ragged coat. I bought new kinds of dog food, special hamburger, yogurt. He was apologetic when he couldn't eat it, his eyes limpid with a plea for understanding, his stiff brush-tail quivering to explain.

"Little Duffer, little black dog—could you try this?" I would ask, offering some tidbit that would surely be irresistible. He would lift his black nose, take it slowly and delicately in his teeth, hold it for a moment hoping I would look away, and then place it on the floor as tactfully as he could. He did not want to disappoint me.

His suffering was a hard thing to watch. He was alone in it, as all creatures, human or animal, are alone in their pain. "The toad beneath the harrow knows exactly where each sharp tooth goes." There is no qualitative or quantitative measurement for pain. It is simply there—sharp or dull, shooting or stabbing, bearable or excruciating, local or general, it is unexplained, uninvited, unavoidable. It takes command. It is all-encompassing, implacable, exigent. But of course I am speaking only of what *I* know of pain. How was it for MacDuff?

He expected no special treatment. He did not pity himself. He took for granted that he would be able to go on about his accustomed terrier business and when he found that it was somehow not working well, he made his own adjustments as unobtrusively as he could. It was still the supreme object of his life to see that *I* was happy. I think he lay under the bush in the rain not in order to wallow in solitary self-pity, but in order that I might not see him in trouble. He liked to please me. He delighted to do my will.

Is animal suffering different from human suffering? I hope so. Animals surely must not suffer the agonies of anxiety which accompany much human pain. "How shall I carry out my duties? What am I to do if this doesn't clear up quickly? Can I bear it if it gets worse?" The element of time is not a philosophical torment to them. They live as we have to be told to live—one day at a time, trustfully. I don't know whether it is accurate to say that "faith" is required of them, but if it is, they fulfill the requirement perfectly. They look to God, the Psalmist tells us, for provision for their needs. They are watched over and cared for by a kind Father. Not the least sparrow falls without his notice. Surely MacDuff was of more value than many sparrows!

I watched him try to lie down on his side, but something obstructed his breathing. When he was asleep he would begin to pant and would waken to change his position, sometimes with little muffled groans. This fellow-creature, I thought, formed by the Hand that formed me, suffers for my sin—for I am of the race of men who brought evil into the world, and without evil there could be no pain, no death. A Scotty would not have had cancer.

His wonderful face—bearded, with tufts of eyebrows springing and black eyes shining—had reminded me of George MacDonald's belief that dogs always behold the face of the Father. MacDuff *knew* things—what did he know? What were the mysteries he saw—too deep or too high or too pure for me to be entrusted with yet? I think they helped him endure the pain. He was not bewildered, of course, by the questions that needle my mind—the origin of evil, God's permission of an animal's or a child's suffering. He was a dog, and to ponder such questions was not required of him. What was required of him he did, in an authentically, thoroughly dog-like style.

I will not weep more for him. I will be thankful for such a gift of grace. He was, I am sure, "assigned" to me. In the sorrow of my late husband's illness, when life seemed a desolate wasteland, MacDuff was there. Jesus, the Bible tells us, during his temptation in the wilderness, was "with the wild beasts." I used to think of that phrase as descriptive of one of the elements of his dereliction, but it may be that the wild beasts, like the angels, *ministered* to him. Is it mere sentimentality to believe that? Is it too much to say that Duffer "ministered" to me? He did. He was my little wild beast in that wilderness.

The Bible does not speak specifically of the destiny of animals but there is a promise in the Letter to the Ephesians which surely must include them, "Everything that exists in heaven or earth shall find its perfection and fulfillment in Christ" (Eph. 1:10 Phillips).

Paul expresses his hope in the eighth chapter of Romans (verse 21 Phillips) "that in the end the whole of created life will be rescued from the tyranny of change and decay, and have its share in that magnificent liberty which can only belong to the children of God!"

Not One Thing Has Failed

I love to read people's journals. Except for one which I was allowed to read in the original handwriting, that of my late husband Jim Elliot, I have had to limit myself to published journals—those, for example of David Brainerd, early missionary to American Indians; Katherine Mansfield, short-story writer from New Zealand; Anne Morrow Lindbergh, wife of the famous pilot; and Mircea Eliade, Rumanian professor of the history of religion at the University of Chicago.

Jim started his journal as a means of self-discipline. He began to get up early in the morning during his junior year in college to read the Bible and pray before classes. He was realistic enough to recognize the slim chances of fitting in any serious study and prayer later in the day. If it had priority on his list of things that mattered, it had to have chronological priority. To see that he did not waste the dearly-bought time, he began to note down on paper specific things he learned from the Word and specific things he asked for in prayer.

"It is not written as a diary of my experiences or feelings," he recorded in his journal, "but as a 'book of remembrance' to enable me to ask definitely by forcing myself to put yearnings into words. All I have asked has not been given and the Father's withholding has served to intensify my desires. . . . He promises water to the thirsty, satiation to the unsatisfied (I do not say *dis*satisfied), filling to the famished for righteousness. So has His concealing of Himself given me longings that can only be slaked when Psalm 17:15 ['As for me I shall behold thy face in righteousness; when I awake I shall be satisfied with beholding thy form'] is realized" (From *The Journals of Jim Elliot*, ed. Elisabeth Elliot. Old Tappan, N.J. : Fleming H. Revell).

"All I have asked has not been given." Not, that is, in the way or at the time he might have predicted. Jim beheld the longed-for Face much sooner than he expected. It is startling to see, from the perspective of nearly thirty years, how much of what he asked *was* given, and given beyond his dreaming.

In his meditations on the Revelation of John, Jim prayed for a greater love for God's church, which he saw "in a shambling ruins," sadly in need of awakening to her calling. "And where shall an overcomer be found? Alas, they all witness that there is no need for overcoming. . . . But Christ was among the churches. The tarnish of the lampstand did not send Him away from them; He is still in their midst. Ah, turn me, Lord Jesus, to see Thee in Thy concern for Thy witness and let me *write*, *publish*, and *send* to the church what things I see."

Knowing Jim and the context in which he wrote, I am

quite certain it was beyond his dreaming to publish a book. He wanted to witness. He wanted to preach. He was called to be a missionary. But he did not imagine himself a published author. The way this came about (his posthumous notoriety) cannot have entered the framework of his prayer.

When Jim prayed for revival he was instructed by reading in David Brainerd's diary how a revival came when Brainerd was sick, discouraged, and cast down, "little expecting that God had chosen the hour of his weakness," Jim wrote, "for manifestation of His strength."

"I visited Indians at Crossweeksung," Brainerd records, "Apprehending that it was my *indispensable duty....* I cannot say I had any hopes of success. I do not know that my hopes respecting the conversion of the Indians were ever reduced to so low an ebb ... yet this was the very season that God saw fittest to begin His glorious work in! And thus He ordained strength out of weakness ... whence I learn that it is good to follow the path of duty, though in the midst of darkness and discouragement."

Following the quotation from David Brainerd Jim includes in the journal a quotation I had sent him from a book which had encouraged me. At that time I was working for the Canadian Sunday School Mission in the bush country of Alberta. My own journal of the first day says, "It is a new and strange experience and I feel keenly my need of the mighty Fortress." On the second day, "I woke at 4:30 with the farm fowl. Made a small breakfast and cleaned up my little home [a fourteen-foot trailer]. In the hot stillness of the afternoon I felt desolate, helpless, lonely, discouraged. Was helped by Deuteronomy 1:29, 30: 'Then I said to you, Do not be in dread or afraid of them. The Lord your God who goes before you will himself fight for you.' "

Jessie Penn-Lewis's book *Thy Hidden Ones* showed me God's purpose in my isolation and helplessness. It was her words I sent in a letter to Jim: "In the Holy Spirit's leading of the soul through the stripping of what may be called 'consecrated self,' and its activity, it is important that there should be a fulfillment of *all outward duty*, that the believer may learn to act on principle rather than on pleasant impulse." It was a spiritual lesson that was to fortify me through countless later experiences when feelings or impulses contributed nothing to an inclination toward obedience. God allows the absence of feeling or, more often, the presence of strong negative feeling that we may simply follow, simply obey, simply trust.

Jim saw, in reading Brainerd, the value of his own journals. He also "was much encouraged to think of a life of godliness in the light of an early death.... Christianity has been analyzed, decried, refused by some; coolly eyed, submitted to, and its forms followed by others who call themselves Christians. But alas, what emptiness in both!

"I have prayed for new men, fiery, reckless men, possessed of uncontrollably youthful passion—these lit by the Spirit of God. I have prayed for new words, explosive, direct, simple words. I have prayed for new miracles. Explaining old miracles will not do. If God is to be known as the God who does wonders in heaven and earth, then God must produce for this generation. Lord, fill preachers and preaching with Thy power. How long dare we go on without tears, without moral passions, hatred and love? Not long, I pray, Lord Jesus, not long." I read these prayers now with awe—new men, new words, new miracles all granted as a result of this young man's death.

The next day, October 28, 1949, when Jim was twenty-two years old he wrote, "He is no fool who gives what he cannot keep to gain what he cannot lose." This was the lesson he found in Luke 16:9, "Make friends for yourself by means of unrighteous mammon, so that when it fails they may receive you into the eternal habitations." The lesson had one application for him in that early morning devotional hour. He did not know how poignantly it would be applied in his life, how aptly illustrated in his death, and how often quoted in the years following.

He wrote in 1953 of watching an Indian die in a jungle house. "And so it will come to me one day, I kept thinking. I wonder if that little phrase I used to use in preaching was something of a prophecy: 'Are you willing to lie in some native hut to die of a disease American doctors never heard of?' I am still willing, Lord God. Whatever You say shall stand at my end time. But oh, I want to live to teach Your word. Lord, let me live 'until I have declared Thy works to this generation.' "

God let him live another three years and then answered that prayer as he answers so many—mysteriously. Five men from a little Stone Age tribe speared him to death. "We thought he had come to eat us," they told me several years later when I had learned their language.

"Why did you think so?" I asked, holding the tiny microphone of a transistor recorder to the mouth of Gikita, the man who seemed to have made the decision to use his spear first.

He laughed. "*Unungi!*" "For no reason. For no particular purpose."

But the God who holds in his hand the breath of every living thing had a purpose. He answered Jim's prayer mysteriously, and "exceedingly abundantly above all" that he had asked or thought. Hundreds, perhaps thousands, of Jim's generation for whom he had prayed were brought to their knees, some of them in lifelong surrender to the call of Christ. Now another generation, born since Jim died, is reading the record of his young manhood—the days which seemed so sterile, so useless, so devoid of any feelings of holiness, when God was at work shaping the character of a man who was to be his witness; the prayers which seemed to go unheard at the time, kept—as all the prayers of all his children are kept, incense for God—and answered after what would have seemed to Jim a long delay.

I think of the farewell message of old Joshua to the elders, heads, judges and officers of Israel: "Be steadfast ... cleave to the Lord ... love the Lord your God. ... You know in your hearts and souls, all of you, that not one thing has failed of all the good things which the Lord your God promised concerning you; all have come to pass for you, not one of them has failed."

On Motherhood and Profanity

OK now, which one of you clowns put that bag of M'n' Ms in the grocery cart?" The mother looks harried.

Two boys, maybe five and seven, eye each other and race away toward the gumball machine near the supermarket door. There is an infant strapped to a plastic board on top of the groceries, and a two year old occupying the built-in child seat in the cart. The mother picks up the M 'n' M candy bag and starts toward the aisle to return it. The two year old screams and she relents, throws the bag in with the rest of her purchases, patiently waits her turn at the check-out, fishes five ten-dollar bills from her purse, receives her small change, and pushing the cart with the babies in it, herds the two boys through the rain to the station wagon in the parking lot.

I go with her in my mind's eye. Jump out in the rain. Open the garage door. Drive in. Close door. Babies, boys, bags into the house—in how many trips? Phone rings. Answer phone, change baby, wipe muddy tracks from kitchen floor. Feed baby, put groceries away, hide M 'n' Ms, start peeling vegetables, take clothes out of dryer, stop fight between two older children, feed two year old, answer phone again, fold clothes, change baby, get boys to:

1) hang up coats,
2) stop teasing two year old,
3) set table.

Light oven, put baby to bed, stop fight, mop up two year old, put chicken in oven, answer phone, put away clothes, finish peeling vegetables, look peaceful and radiant—husband will be home soon.

I see this implacable succession of exigencies in my mind's eye. They come with being a mother. I also see the dreams she dreams sometimes—write a novel, agents call, reviews come in. TV interviews, autograph parties, promotional traveling, a movie contract—preposterous dreams. Try something a little more realistic. Cool modern office, beautiful clothes, make-up and hairdo that stay done all day. A secretarial job perhaps, nothing spectacular, but it's work that actually produces something that doesn't have to be done over at once. It's work that ends at five o'clock. It means something.

I know how it is. I have a mother. I am a mother. I've produced a mother (my daughter, Valerie, has a two year old and expects another child soon). I watched my own mother cope valiantly and efficiently with a brood of six. ("If one child takes all your time," she used to say, "six can't take any more.") We were—we still are—her life. I understand that. Of all the gifts of my life surely those of being somebody's wife and somebody's mother are among the greatest.

But I watch my daughter and other mothers of her generation and I see they have some strikes against them that we didn't have. They have been told insistently and quite persuasively that motherhood is a drag, that tradition is nonsense, that what people have always regarded as "women's work" is meaningless, that "roles" (a word we never bothered much about until a decade or so ago) are changing, that femininity is a mere matter of social conditioning, that it's time to innovate. If the first-grade readers show a picture of a woman driving a hook-and-ladder and a man doing a nurse's job, see what happens to the conditioning. Abolish the stereotypes and we can abolish the myths of masculinity and femininity.

I hear this sort of claptrap, and young mothers often come to me troubled because they can't answer the arguments logically or theologically. They feel, deep in their bones, that there is something terribly twisted about the whole thing but they can't put their finger on what it is.

I think I know what it is. Profanity. Not swearing. I'm not talking about breaking the Third Commandment. I'm talking about treating as meaningless that which is freighted with meaning. Treating as common that which is hallowed. Regarding as a mere triviality what is really a divine design. Profanity is failure to see the inner mystery.

When women—sometimes well-meaning, earnest, truth-seeking ones—say "Get out of the house and do something *creative*, find something *meaningful*, something with more direct access to *reality*," it is a dead giveaway that they have missed the deepest definition of creation, of meaning, of reality. And when you start seeing the world as opaque, that is, as an end in itself instead of as transparent, when you ignore the Other World where this one ultimately finds its meaning, *of course* housekeeping (and any other kind of work if you do it long enough) becomes tedious and empty.

But what have buying groceries, changing diapers and peeling vegetables got to do with *creativity*? Aren't those the very things that keep us from it? Isn't it that kind of drudgery that keeps us in bondage? It's insipid and confining, it's what one conspicuous feminist called "a life of idiotic ritual, full of forebodings and failure." To her I would answer ritual, yes. Idiotic, no, not to the Christian—for although we do the same things anybody else does, and we do them over and over in the same way, the ordinary transactions of everyday life are the very means of transfiguration. It is the common stuff of this world which, because of the Word's having been "made flesh," is shot through with meaning, with charity, with the glory of God.

But this is what we so easily forget. Men as well as women have listened to those quasi-rational claims, have failed to see the fatal fallacy, and have capitulated. Words like personhood, liberation, fulfillment and equality have had a convincing ring and we have not questioned their popular definitions or turned on them the searchlight of Scripture or even of our common sense. We have meekly agreed that the kitchen sink is an obstacle instead of an altar, and we have obediently carried on our shoulders the chips these reductionists have told us to carry.

This is what I mean by profanity. We have forgotten the mystery, the dimension of glory. It was Mary herself who showed it to us so plainly. By the offering up of her physical body to become the God-bearer, she transfigured for all mothers, for all time, the meaning of motherhood. She cradled, fed and bathed her baby—who was very God of very God—so that when we cradle, feed and bathe ours we may see beyond that simple task to the God who in love and humility "dwelt among us and we beheld his glory."

Those who focus only on the drabness of the supermarket, or on the onions or the diapers themselves, haven't an inkling of the mystery that is at stake here, the mystery revealed in the birth of that Baby and consummated on the Cross: *my life for yours.*

The routines of housework and of mothering may be seen as a kind of death, and it is appropriate that they should be, for they offer the chance, day after day, to lay down one's life for others. Then they are no longer routines. By being done with love and offered up to God with praise, they are thereby hallowed as the vessels of the tabernacle were hallowed—not because they were different from other vessels in quality or function, but because they were offered to God. A mother's part in sustaining the life of her children and making it pleasant and comfortable is no triviality. It calls for self-sacrifice and humility, but it is the route, as was the humiliation of Jesus, to glory.

To modern mothers I would say "Let Christ himself be your example as to what your attitude should be. For he, who had always been God by nature, did not cling to his prerogatives as God's equal, but stripped himself of all privilege by consenting to be a slave by nature and being born as a mortal man. And, having become man, he humbled himself by living a life of utter obedience, even to the extent of dying, *and the death he died was the death of a common criminal.* That is why God has now lifted him so high. . ." (Phil. 2:5-11 Phillips).

It is a spiritual principle as far removed from what the world tells us as heaven is removed from hell: If you are willing to lose your life, you'll find it. It is the principle expressed by John Keble in 1822:

If on our daily course our mind
Be set to hallow all we find,
New treasures still, of countless price,
God will provide for sacrifice.

CHRISTIAN HERALD ASSOCIATION AND ITS MINISTRIES

CHRISTIAN HERALD ASSOCIATION, founded in 1878, publishes The Christian Herald Magazine, one of the leading interdenominational religious monthlies in America. Through its wide circulation, it brings inspiring articles and the latest news of religious developments to many families. From the magazine's pages came the initiative for CHRISTIAN HERALD CHILDREN'S HOME and THE BOWERY MISSION, two individually supported not-for-profit corporations.

CHRISTIAN HERALD CHILDREN'S HOME, established in 1894, is the name for a unique and dynamic ministry to disadvantaged children, offering hope and opportunities which would not otherwise be available for reasons of poverty and neglect. The goal is to develop each child's potential and to demonstrate Christian compassion and understanding to children in need.

Mont Lawn is a permanent camp located in Bushkill, Pennsylvania. It is the focal point of a ministry which provides a healthful "vacation with a purpose" to children who without it would be confined to the streets of the city. Up to 1000 children between the ages of 7 and 11 come to Mont Lawn each year.

Christian Herald Children's Home maintains year-round contact with children by means of an *In-City Youth Ministry*. Central to its philosophy is the belief that only through sustained relationships and demonstrated concern can individual lives be truly enriched. Special emphasis is on individual guidance, spiritual and family counseling and tutoring. This follow-up ministry to inner-city children culminates for many in financial assistance toward higher education and career counseling.

THE BOWERY MISSION, located at 227 Bowery, New York City, has since 1879 been reaching out to the lost men on the Bowery, offering them what could be their last chance to rebuild their lives. Every man is fed, clothed and ministered to. Countless numbers have entered the 90-day residential rehabilitation program at the Bowery Mission. A concentrated ministry of counseling, medical care, nutrition therapy, Bible study and Gospel services awakens a man to spiritual renewal within himself.

These ministries are supported solely by the voluntary contributions of individuals and by legacies and bequests. Contributions are tax deductible. Checks should be made out either to CHRISTIAN HERALD CHILDREN'S HOME or to THE BOWERY MISSION.

Administrative Office: 40 Overlook Drive, Chappaqua, New York 10514
Telephone: (914) 769-9000